DEATH DANCE

A True Story of Drug Addiction and Redemption

BY CLIFFORD HARRIS

as told to Patrice Thomas Conwell

Harris, Clifford
Conwell, Patrice Thomas
    DeathDance / by Clifford Harris
                as told to Patrice Thomas Conwell

ISBN 0-9670450-0-2

*Some names have been changed by request for privacy.

Scripture references in this book are from the *New
International Version* of the Holy Bible.

FOREWORD

Deep within me I am convinced that the Holy Spirit has compelled me to share my life story with you. Many of my Christian friends have discouraged me from revealing the "naked truth" of my life which is not a pretty picture nor complimentary, to say the least.

However, I am impressed to tell you about my closest, personal friend, Jesus Christ, who loved and protected me when I wasn't even thinking about Him. His love for me has been so overwhelming, I want you to know what He has done for me despite my sins.

The Bible is a source of encouragement and comfort for sinners. Note the graphic description of David's act of adultery and murder as recorded in 2 Samuel 11 and 12. By recounting his sin, repentance and hope of pardon through the mercy of God, in the presence of the court, priests, judges, princes and men of war, David preserved to the latest generation the knowledge of his fall. Instead of endeavoring to conceal his guilt, he desired that others might be instructed by the sad history of his fall. (see *Patriarchs and Prophets*, pp. 725-726)

God called David "a man after mine own heart." (Acts 13:22) God also knows my heart: my selfishness, dishonesty, temper, disrespect, adultery, lying, stealing and jealousy. If God forgave and saved David, I know that He will forgive and save me and everyone whose repentance is sincere and profound like David's. It doesn't matter what degree of sin you might be experiencing, only Jesus can save you.

The biblical record of David is one to which I can relate. My prayer is that someone will give their heart to Jesus Christ and experience the miracle of conversion as I have.

Before reading this book, please pray and ask the Holy Spirit to give you an open mind to understand how it can help multitudes of people come to Christ. Just as Satan tempts, traps and terminates unsuspecting victims on life's highway, Christ rescues, redeems and restores those entangled in the ugliness of evil. The graphic details outlined herein are intended, by contrast, to glorify the Creator who transforms men and women by the power of His love and grace.

—Cliff Harris

CONTENTS

DEDICATION

To my children, Stephen, Jeffrey, Rhonda and their mother, Evelyn, who have demonstrated God's love by forgiving and loving me despite all the pain, heartache and misery I brought into their lives. My personal gift from God is that none of them has ever used drugs. "Thanks" seems so inadequate to say to the four of them.

It is my hope that this story will help families of drug addicts follow the example of my children and their mother in exhibiting the forgiveness and love of Christ.

PROLOGUE

The man that I have the privilege of presenting to you today has a long history of success in his field," Freddie said, as she introduced me at a California church in 1988. "First, he is an honor graduate of Colorado State Penitentiary, having received his bachelor's degree in burglary in 1977. He returned in 1983 and received his master's degree in larceny on January 3, 1984. Prior to completing his higher education, he enrolled in numerous institutions, including Denver County Jail, Arapaho County Jail, Adams County Jail, Lake Alford County Jail and Long Beach County Jail. His elementary schooling included Dallas City Jail, Oberlin, Ohio City Jail, Denver City Jail and Aurora City Jail."

Memories spilled over me as I listened to Freddie introduce me and continue her list of names and places. Yes, I remembered. In fact, I remembered those places too well. They reminded me of the years I had wasted, and the mess I had made of my life.

"His professional experiences," she went on to say, "includes ten years as a heroin addict, eight years as a cocaine addict, twenty years of marijuana use and five years of amphetamines and barbiturates. His direct experiences include robbery, direct IV injection, burglary, extortion, assault and battery, larceny, contempt of court, trespassing, and possession of narcotics."

What a wasted life, I thought. And that could've been the end of my story—except then she added as she closed, " He

3

comes to you today, as a new creature in Christ with five years of sobriety, a new wife and family, owner of a new home, and president of Drug Alternative Program."

She pause and said, "Mr. Cliff Harris."

People applauded, laughed, and cheered. My wife had given me the best introduction I've ever had.

Behind that brief snapshot, however, lay years of pain, years of guilt. Most of all, years of regret.

This is my story, the best that I remember it.

Drugs have affected my memory, so a few things aren't totally clear. I'm not positive I have everything in the proper time sequence. Despite that, I want to tell you my story—the true story of a man who sank to the depths of human hell, but then arose, by God's grace to a new and happy life.

Chapter 1

A GOOD HOME

"Clifford?"

I immediately knew from the tone of my mother's voice that I was in trouble—again. I wanted to pretend like I didn't hear her calling me. Crouched down behind the chicken shack, my mind churned as I tried to decide what to do.

"Clifford? If you hear me callin' you, you better get in here right now."

If I didn't go, I'd be in worse trouble than I already was. I straightened up from my crouched position. My knees ached from being bent so long. With deliberate steps I walked to the house, trying to delay the wrath awaiting me.

"Yes mama?" I said haltingly. I tried to put on my best I-don't-know-why-you-called-me-in-here-I'm-innocent face; eyes wide, eyebrows raised, and a question-mark expression. Mama stood with her hands firmly planted on her fleshy hips.

"What's this I hear about you throwin' rocks at the neighbor?"

"What mama? What you mean?" I tried to stall the inevitable. I knew the neighbor had already filled mama in with the details and she just wanted to hear it from my mouth.

"You know what I mean, Clifford. Were you throwin' rocks at the neighbor?"

My mind replayed the scene. Our neighbor was hanging her fresh-washed clothes on the line. For some unexplainable reason, I decided to mess with her a little bit.

I stuffed a handful of rocks in my pants pocket, and climbed onto our garage roof. When I had my target in good eyesight, I took careful aim and launched a rock toward my neighbor's back.

"Ping." The small stone hit the target, pouncing off to the ground. As soon as it hit, I ducked down, my body flattened to the roof with my head up just high enough to sneak a peek. The neighbor whirled around, a puzzled look on her face. Seeing nothing, she turned back to hanging her wash.

"Ping." I threw another stone, and she whirled around, her brows furrowed together in an angry look. Each time I threw a stone, her face got angrier and angrier from not being able to tell where the attack was coming from. I got cockier with each successful throw. I knew she'd never figure out to look toward the roof.

"Ping." I threw another stone, but I didn't duck fast enough. Big mistake.

"CLIFFORD HARRIS." Her voice thundered across the field. "I'M GONNA TELL YOUR MAMA."

Panic stricken, I leaped off the garage roof and ran across the field straight to her.

"Oh please don't tell my mama, "I begged. "I'm sorry. I'm really sorry."

"Well you should be sorry, 'cause that was a mean thing to do."

I pleaded with her not to tell mama, because I knew mama would set my hind parts on fire. But my pleading fell on deaf ears. And now here I was standing in front of my mama, withering from the look on her face. Her voice pierced my reflections.

"I asked you a question, Clifford. Were you throwin' rocks at the neighbor?"

"Yes ma'am." My voice was small as the answer squeaked out. There was no need to lie. That would only make my whipping worse. And thank goodness—'cause the whipping I got was mighty bad enough.

"Now go on and get outta here my little bad boy," mama said as she whacked me on the backside. "And don't let the screen door..." CRASH!! The wooden screen door cracked against the door frame as I bolted back outside.

It was Jacksonville, Florida. I was born on January 31, 1940 the fifth child of seven children born to George and Louise Harris. Daddy was a good looking man of medium height, with skin as brown as dark chocolate and smooth as a block of ice. He had stone chiseled features and piercing brown eyes.

Mama was an inch taller than daddy. She had butterscotch colored skin, straight, dark brown hair, and high cheekbones that reflected her Indian roots. She loved being around people—entertaining and spinning stories about her childhood. I could sit for hours, fascinated as she talked about her life as a little girl and all the mischievous things she did. She reminded me of me.

There were six kids living, seven altogether. My brothers, Ronald, Melvin and Gene were so much older than me, I don't remember much about them growing up. Ronald died when he was 18, Melvin left to join the army when I was six years old, and Gene was just too old for me to play with.

My tattle tale sister, Melba, was the main instigator of all my whippings, though that didn't stand in the way of us being close. And baby sister Sandra was the child everyone said mama was keeping for White people, because of her fair skin and curly hair.

We were considered a middle class Black family. We had a

nice house with a fireplace in the living room, though we didn't have a bathroom inside. But the day we got a bathroom inside was a shoutin' time.

From a small boy I noticed everything about me seemed different. Sometimes I'd stand real still and just stare at myself in the mirror, intently soaking in the differences between me and my brothers and sisters. I'd feel my skin. I'd touch my hair.

My skin was dark brown like daddy's, and my hair was cotton soft and tightly curled like coiled wire. All my brothers and sisters were varying shades of lighter brown, some with hazel eyes and light brown eyes, and all with wavy straight hair.

"Clifford, are you adopted?" I'd softly whisper to the face staring back at me in the mirror. "You got to be 'cause you don't look like anybody else in the family."

My feelings of being different intensified when family members referred to me as "the ugly boy." I don't know who started the name, but it became an inside family joke among everybody—my parents, brothers, sisters, aunts, uncles, cousins—everybody. Each time I heard "he's the ugly boy," or "hey ugly boy," the words would sear into my brain, sending my thoughts into a jumble of confusion and stinging my self esteem.

Deep inside I knew my family was just teasing. But I saw how the light skinned, straight haired Blacks seemed to get better treatment from the Whites in town, and from other Blacks as well. I could tell that the lighter your skin and the straighter your hair, the better looking you were thought to be. So if my own family considered me the "ugly boy," what did that mean about people outside of my family? Surely they were thinking the same thing, only they weren't teasing.

Besides looking different, I acted different too. I was a big prankster, constantly acting up just to get a laugh. Like the time mama was ironing clothes and heard the dog yapping uncontrollably.

"My goodness. What's the matter with that dog, making all that noise?"

Without really looking up from what I was doing, I shrugged my shoulders and said, "He bit me, so I bit him back."

When I wasn't pulling pranks, it seemed I could never do the right thing. So often mama had to whip and scold me. "Goodness Clifford," she would heave out in exasperation, "you're the worst child I have." Little by little, I believed her.

————•————

Mama and daddy were devout Seventh day Adventist Christians. Their biblical convictions didn't just surface on the day we went to church. It defined the way we lived our lives.

Our parents taught us to be loving, honest, and respectful to God and to everyone around us. There was no alcohol drinking, card playing, gambling, cussing, rock 'n roll, or wild parties in our house or the houses of anyone else we knew. I guess that's because everyone else we knew was Seventh Day Adventist also.

"Clifford, time to get up for worship," was an everyday phrase my father bellowed in the mornings before he left for work. I'd stumble in the living room and find my spot on the couch between Melba and Sandra. Daddy would give a devotional reading and then we'd close worship with prayer.

After worship, daddy was on his way out the door and mama got the rest of us started for the day. This ritual marked the beginning of each day, and Friday marked the start of a different ritual—preparing for Sabbath.

Friday was called "preparation day" because it was the day all the house cleaning and cooking was done because we didn't do any work on Sabbath.

"Mama, why I got to dust the furniture? Can't Melba do that?" I'd drone and complain about the chores I'd have to do. Seems like the house got extra dirty right before the Sabbath, making the cleaning more burdensome than any other time during the week.

"No, Melba is helping me cook. Now stop complaining and do what you're told."

I'd take my rag and rub around on the big pieces of furniture first, tackling all the little ledges and crevices second. I didn't dare skip any spot 'cause if Mama found it, I'd just have to come back and do it all over again. All the while I muttered to myself, in my head, while the house pulsated with activities of preparation day.

Soon, the air bloomed with fragrances coming from the kitchen, and the house was overcome with smells of food for Sabbath's dinner. Mama always cooked a banquet feast for us to enjoy after church.

As I did my Friday chores, my mouth became a river of anticipation, my saliva glands involuntarily responding to the smells enveloping me. It was absolute torture knowing that none of that food would pass my lips until Saturday afternoon.

By sundown Friday night, the house gleamed like polished brass. Us kids did too, after taking baths and putting on crisp pajamas. As the sun began falling from the sky, my sister Melba would sit down at the piano and start playing songs. On Friday night we did a lot of singing, each one taking a turn suggesting a favorite selection. Week after week when it was daddy's turn to pick a song, he never wavered from his one and only choice "Day Is Dying in the West." Never a Friday evening went by that we didn't sing that song. To this day, I can sing each verse which has been burned into my memory.

Saturday morning, the family was up early putting on their best clothes and faces for church. Spit polished shoes, hard creased pants, flowing dresses, and sassy hats.

Before we left, mama fortified us with her fried grits with white beans. She'd cook up a pot of grits, let them cool, then fry them in a skillet. For the finishing touch, she'd pour white beans over them. With full bellies, we went to church to get our Sabbath blessing.

I enjoyed going to church, mostly because I got to see my friends. After church was even more fun, though. Our house filled up, practically bursting at the seams with uncles, aunts and cousins who came to enjoy mama's cooking and each other's company.

Few Sabbath experiences competed with the ecstasy of finally being able to sink my teeth into collard greens, fried chicken, macaroni and cheese, potatoes, rolls— you name it, we probably had it.

No food went to waste. People even vied for the honor of drinking the "pot liquor"—the juice left in the pot from the greens or other vegetables. Then the smackin' lips would start and somebody would say "Oooooo Louise, you stuck your foot in that food, girl."

All the adults sat around stuffed from head to toe with mama's fine cooking, content to relax and talk, or fall asleep while Sabbath afternoon droned on. I, on the other hand, was anxious for Sabbath to end.

Back and forth, back and forth I'd run to mama asking, "Mama, is Sabbath over yet?" "Now Clifford," she'd say, "you know Sabbath's not over until the sun goes down."

After dinner, Sabbath just seemed to stand still. Although us kids were allowed to go outside and entertain ourselves, we couldn't really like we did during the rest of the week. So after a couple of hours of listening to Bible stories, playing Bible games, or just horsing around, there was nothing left for a little kid to do, except sit around and be bored.

I'd let hours go by before I dared to go back to mama and ask, "Is it over yet?"

"Clifford, you just asked me that five minutes ago. Now don't ask me again. When you see it getting dark outside, then you'll know that Sabbath is over."

Thank goodness for the winter months when the sun set early and let me get back to the business of fun.

————•————

Sunday was a free day. After worship and breakfast everybody was free to do what they wanted, except for daddy. He always went to work.

Daddy was a brick mason, a common trade for Black men in those days. All of daddy and mama's brothers laid brick. Back then, brick masons were the highest paid workers on a construction job. They made more money than the plumber or the electrician.

Daddy earned a good living as a brick mason, but he always worked, even when the family went on vacation. He never went anywhere without his tools.
Sometimes I'd try to interest him in something other than work. Like, spending time with me.

"Daddy, can we play baseball?" I earnestly stared into his face. "No son," he replied shaking his head, "I have to go to work."

"Aw daddy, come on please? Just this once?" I added a little more of a pleading tone.

"I said no, son."

Daddy's refusal seemed cold and callous, and a direct rejection of me. It hurt me that he would rather work on Sunday than spend time with me. I wanted him to feel just as hurt and rejected as I did. But I wouldn't dare speak out loud the thoughts that were running through my head. I sulked away, feeling sorry for myself.

"What's the matter with you Clifford?" mama asked.

"All daddy does is work, work, work. He never spends any time with me or anybody else in this family." My pent up frustrations spewed out like a volcano. "All he does is eat and sleep here. He thinks more about his tools than he does his own kids. What kind of daddy is that?"

"The kind of daddy who makes sure you got food on the table, clothes to cover your body, a roof over your head, and a bed for you to sleep in." Mama's voice was understanding yet firm. "He don't have time to play when there's a family to provide for. It's a man's responsibility to take care of his wife and children. To support them. You watch your daddy. He is showin' you what it means to be a good man."

I was embarrassed by my selfishness. All that hard work daddy was doing, he was doing for me.

And when more work became available in Oberlin, Ohio than in Jacksonville, Daddy packed us up and moved the family to join mama's brother, Luther, who was already working there.

I was eight years old.

My son, pay attention to what I say;
listen closely to my words.
Do not let them out of your sight, keep
them within your heart; for they are life to
those who find them and health to a man's
whole body.
Proverbs 4:20-22

Chapter 2

THE TRADE

Oberlin, Ohio was a small college town. All the Whites lived on one side and all the Blacks lived on the other. One bank and maybe two police cars served the whole town. And looking through my child's eye, there seemed to be more bikes than cars.

Daddy's business started booming and he had to hire men in the community to work with him. My brothers worked with him too. It was important to daddy that his sons learn the brick mason trade as preparation for being able to provide for themselves, and later, their families. So when my brothers turned sixteen, daddy took them out of school and they worked alongside him full time.

Education was not a top priority for Blacks at that time. Having money making skills that enabled a Black man to provide for his family was much more important. Once I remember hearing daddy say "When you get a college degree, what good is that? You aren't going to get a job as a professor, so why do you need college?" Blacks with a high school or college education didn't have the professional opportunities that exist today.

During the summer of 1952, when I was twelve years old, daddy decided that I needed to begin learning "the trade" as well. My oldest brother, Melvin, had gotten so good, he and daddy were working as business partners. Now it was time to bring me into the fold. I eagerly awaited the first morning of my going to work.

"Clifford, come on. It's time to get up," rang daddy's familiar morning greeting. But this morning had a different meaning. I was joining the ranks of men, working a real job side by side with daddy, my brother, Melvin, and other adults. Real men.

I eagerly jumped into my clothes, making it to family worship in record time. When it was time to go, mama handed daddy his packed lunch as she did each morning. Then she turned around with another lunch and held it out to me. As I accepted this offering into my hands, I sensed I was crossing the gulf that separates boy from man.

"Everybody, this here's my son Clifford," daddy said, introducing me to the other workers once we arrived at the job site. "He's going to be working with us during the summer learning the trade." The men smiled at me in comradely approval.

The crew was in the process of building a cement block wall basement. When the truck delivered the cement blocks, everybody helped slide the blocks down a plank into the basement. Then the blocks had to be stacked.

I carried each 12 inch concrete block to its resting place, where they sat until I carried each to the men as they built the wall. As the Ohio sun rose high in the noon sky, it got scorching hot. The heat drained my strength so that each block felt as though it would pull my arms out of socket. My work day didn't end soon enough.

"How was your first day?" mama asked as I limped through the door that evening. I don't think she needed a verbal answer. My body language spoke volumes, loud and clear. Every muscle screamed its displeasure. I felt like the sun had stolen all my energy to fuel its bright warmth.

Each day I was forced back on the job, I despised a little bit more. I discovered it was hard work being a man. And painful.

I didn't want to be a man anymore. I just wanted to be a kid. And like any kid my age, I wanted to stay home and play with my friends around the neighborhood. Why did I have to learn this trade anyway? Laying brick wasn't the only way a man could make money.

Finally, one day on the job site, resentment overwhelmed my good sense. As daddy was talking about the value of learning the trade, I began arguing with him. I found myself getting no where in defense of not learning this trade.

"Well I don't want to be a bricklayer," I spat out in disgust. If there was one final reason not to learn the trade, that was it. "I want to be a taxi cab driver."

Daddy scraped off the trowel he was using and whacked my behind.

"I'm going to teach you this trade," he said in a this-is-the-end-of-the-discussion tone. "You may grow old, but you won't be able to say I never taught you anything."

With that, he turned back to his work. I did the same. We never discussed it again.

Each week, I got paid along with the other workers. I had to pay mama five dollars for the lunch she packed everyday, and like daddy, I put ten percent aside for tithe. The rest of the money was mine to spend however I wanted.

One day I overheard some of the guys talking at work.

"Hey, you going over to James' house?"

"What's happening at James' house?"

"Maaannn, we got a lil' craps game goin'. You know, we shoot some dice for a small wager and stuff. You should come on over and join us."

"Can anybody come?"

"Sure man. If you got the dough, you can blow. We don't turn nobody away who's bringing cash."

17

I had never seen anyone gamble in my life. The mystery of it intrigued me and the guys talked as if James' house was the hottest thing going. The next payday, I went around to James' house—just to watch. I heard loud whooping and hollering even before I got to the door.

Stepping inside I saw about four or five men kneeling on the floor in a semicircle in front of a wall. While my eyes adjusted to the dimness, I vaguely saw heads bent toward the floor. Intent on what they were doing, I didn't think anybody noticed when I came in.

"Aaawww come on baby. Work for daddy," a voice said.

I edged closer to get a better look. Peeping over their backs, I saw a man facing the wall shaking cupped hands furiously. Periodically, he stopped shaking long enough to put his hands up to his mouth and blow on them.

As he flung his hands out toward the wall a loud "HAA" gurgled from his throat, as though he was pronouncing a Pentecostal blessing. Two little white cubes with black dots flew out into the air and hit the wall, landing on the floor. Immediately the circle exploded with yells of triumph, clapping, laughter, and groans of despair. The man who'd thrown the dice took money from everybody else in the circle.

This went on and on, each man in the circle having his turn throwing the dice; one dollar bills, five dollar bills, and sometimes ten dollar bills, exchanged hand to hand. I watched in utter fascination, as if in a trance, hypnotized by the excitement generated by the circle. My feet felt bolted to the floor, unable to move. I sensed I had walked into the forbidden, but I couldn't leave.

I don't know what attracted me most; the animation of the winner's triumph clashing with the losers' agony with equal force, or their silent acceptance of me, a kid, into the adult inner circle. I watched for a few more minutes, then just couldn't hold back any longer.

"Can I play?" the words spilled from my lips.

Five pairs of eyes looked in my direction, staring into my eager face.

"You got any money?" James asked.

I gleefully held up a fistful of dollar bills, my week's pay. James did a quick cut-away glance to a man kneeling across from him, a smile slowly creeping across his face.

"S-s-h-h-ure, you come on here. You can play just like the rest of us," James replied.

I was so elated, I didn't notice the men stealing glances at each other, hunching each other in the sides with their elbows, tempering their wide smiles to smirks. I'm sure they were practically drooling in anticipation of the easy money they were about to make. I had "SUCKER" written across my forehead. Only I didn't see it.

"Here," James gestured. "Kneel right in front of the wall."

I knelt down. All the men gathered around me.

"To get the dice you gotta lay down some money," James instructed.

I laid down one dollar. Since I was just learning the game I didn't want to spend too much money at once.

"I'll fade it," somebody said and laid a dollar on top of mine.

"Okay here's the dice." James handed me the cubes. "Now throw them against the wall and see what you get."

Taking the dice into my hands I did what I'd seen them do. I shook my hands furiously and with great confidence. Flinging my hands out, I turned the dice loose and let out a big "HAA!" The dice hit the ground.

"You got an eight. Now who's gonna bet that Clifford here can throw another eight."

"I bet five dollars he can't," said one man, throwing five dollars on the ground on top of my money.

Everybody else bet against me too, and threw their money down. I took the dice, shook them furiously, turned them loose and let out a bigger "HAA."

I got a six.

The men let out whoops of laughter and slaps on the back.

"Sorry kid, you lose." James picked up the money pile and divided it among everybody.

"Let me try again," I said confidently.

"Well, you gotta put more money down." I laid down another dollar.

"Aw come on Clifford, you can put more down than that. What, you a scardy cat or something? All you need is one good throw. This might be it."

I put down a few more dollars and took the dice. They yelled encouragement while I went through the shaking, blowing process. When the dice hit the floor the men exploded in yells and laughter, slapping each other on the shoulder.

I lost AGAIN.

"Come on Clifford, try it one more time," somebody yelled.

I did and I lost. And I kept on losing.

As my money quickly dwindled, I was aching for just one win. All I needed was one. I shook the dice with determined gusto and let them fly. They hit the floor and I yelled in delight, arching my body up and holding my hands to the sky. I'd won!

"Hey, alright Clifford," someone said as a couple of guys slapped me on the back. I excitedly took the pile of dollars on the floor. That win was all I needed to get the blood rushing through my veins. I couldn't give the dice up. And the guys kept encouraging me, saying that I was on a roll.

I hadn't watched the game long enough in the beginning to know they were cheating me. I didn't know that once you had the dice and established points, you could throw as many times as you wanted until you threw a three or seven. Once you threw a three or seven, you lost. As many times as you threw your first number before hitting a three or seven, you won. These guys were making me pay each time I threw the dice. And I never questioned them. If they said I lost, I just accepted it.

It didn't take long before I was totally out of money. As I lost my last dollar, an awful realization crashed over my head. I'd lost my entire paycheck, including mama's five dollars AND God's tithe. I needed to find a way to get it all back. Besides, I wanted to keep playing with the guys.

"You all outta cash little man?" James asked. "Cause if you outta cash, you got to go."

I looked into his matter of fact face.

"I'll be right back. Save my spot," I said as the screen door almost caught me on the backside on my way out.

I ran out of James' house at break neck speed and started for home. Nearing the door to my house, I slowed to a trot, then tiptoed inside. Looking to see if mama was anywhere nearby, I gingerly picked my way to her bedroom. I couldn't let her see me or she'd ask what I was doing home. I side stepped the floor's creaky spots, peeking around corners and glancing behind me to make sure she wasn't close by.

I knew daddy kept money in the dresser drawer. All the kids knew it and he knew we knew it, but it didn't matter. He never worried about us taking it because that was stealing, and we didn't steal.

My heart pounding in my chest, I walked closer and closer to mama and daddy's dresser drawer. Choking back the fear of being discovered, I slowly pulled the drawer out until a wad of bills, tucked in the corner, came into view . I'm not sure how much money was there—maybe close to three hundred dollars.

Taking twenty dollars, I shut the drawer. Daddy would never miss just twenty dollars. Besides, I would replace it after winning back all the money I'd lost. So I was really just borrowing it for a while.

I snuck out of the house and ran back to James'.

"Here," I panted and flopped back into the circle. "Here's some more money so I can keep playing."

The guys whistled and clapped, and the dice continued to roll.

It only took a few minutes before the twenty was gone. If I had been thinking clearly, that would have been a huge clue I was never going to win enough to get all my money back. But the guys kept teasing me and encouraging me to throw one more time. Just one more time. That's all I needed—one more throw to win it all back.

So, I went home again and took more money from mama and daddy's drawer. I must have made that trip home three or four times, taking a little more money each time. On the last trip, I grabbed all of the money left in the drawer. Even then, I shook off the guilt by promising myself I would win and use the money to replace all I had taken.

I lost EVERY dollar.

Sitting facing the wall, I was paralyzed. Staring at the faces looking at me, reality struck me like a bolt of lightening . I was never getting that money back. I was embarrassed that I couldn't hang with the men. My manly facade was broken, exposing the child I really was. The consequences looming before me brought terror to my heart.

"You're out Clifford," someone said, shoving me out of the

circle.

With urgent pleading, I objected.

"But I know I can win..."

"YOU'RE OUT," James thundered at me. The warm smile that had invited me into the game was replaced by stone cold anger flashing from his eyes.

"Get on outta here RIGHT NOW!" His language was spiked with words I knew were considered filthy and he shoved me toward the door.

Each step toward home hammered into my head the magnitude of what I had really done. I had lost all of my money, gambling—a direct contradiction to everything my parents had taught me. And not only had I lost MY money; I had stolen their's and lost it as well. There was no way to replace it, and it would be missed. As I stepped inside the house, daddy was waiting for me.

"Clifford, I went into my dresser drawer to get something and I noticed my money missing. Sandra couldn't have done it 'cause she's too little to reach the drawer, and Melba wouldn't have done it." Then came the punch line. "Did you take the money out of my drawer?"

My heart stopped. It must have, because I don't remember breathing. As daddy waited for an answer, I could reach out and touch the silence hanging between us. My face got hot and tingly, and my mouth felt like it was stuffed with a huge wad of cotton.

"Clifford," daddy said slowly, softly, puncturing the silence. "Did you take the money from the drawer?"

It may have seemed easy for me to steal, but I couldn't lie. Neither could I pry my mouth open to say anything. So I nodded my head yes.

"*WHAT IN THE WORLD* DID YOU USE *THA-REE HUN-*

DRED DOLL-ARS FOR?!"

I trembled from his harsh voice. Shame washed over me. Guilt ripped my heart. Though petrified of what daddy would do to me if I told him what I had done with the money, I felt backed into a corner with no way to get out.

"Come on, you'd better talk to me son."

"I shot dice," I whispered. The squeaky voice didn't sound like it came from my body.

"You did WHAT?" Incredulous disbelief lit up daddy's face and then faded into grave disappointment.

The dam broke and sobs convulsed my body.

"I didn't... mean to take... your money. I didn't mean to. I was just... borrowing it. I was going to win... it... all... back."

Daddy demanded to know where I was. The whole story gushed from my lips in rushing torrents. When the torrents dried up, I felt pathetic. Daddy just shook his head and sighed.

"Clifford" (big pause) "they stole your money. You were just a kid they could take advantage of."

I stood in my spot, waiting for the inevitable. Waiting to be told to commence with my part of the ritual—going outside to the big elm tree and cutting a switch that daddy could use to commence with his part of the ritual—whipping my tail. But he stepped around me and walked out of the house.

A little while later, daddy returned with every dollar that I had been cheated out of. Without saying a word to me, he put the money back in the drawer and never talked about it again.

I would have felt better if he had whipped me. This was one time, I knew without a doubt, I deserved it. Instead, getting no whipping left an unresolved pain of disappointment I'd inflicted on my father. A pain I felt so intensely, that I never stole from him, or mama, again.

If *anyone does not provide for his relatives, and especially for his immediate family, he has denied the faith and is worse than an unbeliever.*

1 Timothy 5:8

Chapter 3

SCHOOL DAYS

My early education held no real significance for me until high school. I completed kindergarten through fourth grade in an Adventist school in Florida. In Oberlin, I attended an integrated public school and encountered my first personal brush with prejudice. The teachers in that school didn't care if I learned or not. As a result, I didn't really care either.

My school life changed drastically after my eighth grade graduation.

"Clifford, your mother and I have decided to send you to Pine Forge Institute for high school starting this coming term." Daddy's revelation was a statement of finality rather than one inviting my opinion.

Pine Forge Institute (now Pine Forge Academy) is an all-Black Adventist boarding school located in Pine Forge, Pennsylvania, next to Pottstown. Because Christian education is a strong value among Adventists, Black Adventists who could afford it sent their kids to Pine Forge, and my parents were no different.

"I don't want to go to Pine Forge," I replied feeling obligated to myself to assert my opinion. Going to Pine Forge meant leaving home and I had never been away from home. The very idea put butterflies in my stomach.

But that wasn't the real reason I didn't want to go. I really didn't want to go because I was scared I was too dumb. School hadn't been too kind to me up to this point, so I hadn't been a good student. If I went away to Pine Forge, I felt the other kids would be smarter than me and make fun of how uneducated I was. I couldn't let that happen.

"Clifford, we are sending you to Pine Forge, period."

" Fine. You can send me, but you can't make me stay. I'll just do something bad when I get there so they'll have to send me back home."

In my half-hearted attempt to assert myself, I was honest enough to divulge a plan whereby I wouldn't have to stay away from home. It was not a plan, however, that won approval from my parents.

"You try that, Clifford, and you'll wish you had just stayed here," daddy said with his "don't mess with me" stern voice.

"You're going to Pine Forge. And YOU'RE GOING to be good." End of discussion.

So in 1955 I entered the ninth grade at Pine Forge.

The Pine Forge campus is nestled in the Pennsylvania hills, isolated from the closest town. I roomed with three other boys in the boys' dormitory located on the other side of the campus, far away from the girls' dormitory.

The school is totally self-contained, offering all the necessities for student living, including lots of rules to help students maintain clean, moral, Christian behavior. To teenagers, one rule is too many.

The stricter rules were the ones that governed how boys and girls related to each other. The school administration did everything possible to stop budding romances between students. But nothing could stop me when I saw Eloise.

Two of my roommates ran with a clique from Philadelphia. Eloise was part of that group, and she was the prettiest girl I had ever seen in my life. She had big brown eyes and a smile that made her face glow. When she spoke, her voice was so soft and sweet, my heart melted. I loved princess-style dresses, and she wore them better than any other girl, showing off her small waistline. I was in love. Unfortunately, I was on a one-way street.

Although we ran in the same group, Eloise didn't return my intense interest. Undaunted, I relentlessly pursued her—never looking to the right or the left to see if there were any other girls looking my way. As far as I was concerned, Eloise was the only one for me and everybody on campus knew it. It took months, but she finally came around. And when she did, we became a couple.

One of the school's "keep the boys away from the girls" rules in my time was no co-ed seating during meals in the cafeteria, or in church service. The boys ate on one side of the cafe, and the girls on the other. To me, it was cruel and unusual punishment to have to sit apart from Eloise everyday.

At every meal, I silently wished I could set my tray right down next to Eloise's and stare into those beautiful brown eyes. I just wanted to be around her, look at her, talk to her. Finally, I couldn't take it anymore. I decided that despite the rules, I was going to eat lunch with Eloise anyway.

On the day of attack, I strode into the cafeteria with a determined walk. Determined to defend my right to be with the girl I loved. My heart felt it would bust through my shirt as I got my food. Slowly, I turned around. I knew my buddies were waiting for me at our usual table. But fixing my eyes on Eloise's table, I walked right past my friends. Not moving my head to the left or right, I marched through the boys' dining side straight over to the girls' section. Straight to Eloise.

"Hi there." I faked the cool tone of someone who was calm and unruffled.

29

I put my tray down on the table across from Eloise. Immediately, all talking in the cafeteria stopped. Time stood still. I didn't look around, but I could feel eyes burning through the back of my shirt. Eloise's eyes were round saucers, her mouth hanging open and her face flushed a rosy hue.

"Clifford." Eloise shouted in a whisper. "What are you doing?"

Her body hunched across the table as she tried to get as close to me as she dared, trying not to bring attention to herself or me. Her expression was a mixture of seriousness, fright, and pleasure. She didn't say so, but I think she liked my breaking the rules just to be with her.

Within three seconds, before a sound could pass my lips, the hairs on the back of my neck stood up, saluting the presence I felt behind me. I turned to see "Lefty," the head cook standing there.

Lefty's real name was Mrs. Hardy, but because of a foot problem that made her look like she had two left feet, the students called her Lefty behind her back. Well, it didn't take Lefty long to address the situation.

"You know it's against the rules for you to sit at the girls' table, Clifford. You'd better get yourself, and that tray, back on the side where you belong."

The fight for love had just turned into a fight for honor and pride as well. Mostly pride.

"I want to sit here, and I'm going to sit here. I don't see anything wrong with us just sitting together."

"Fine. You sit there. And I'll go call Elder Watson."

As the words hung in the air a faint tremor flicked the core of my insides.

"Fine. You call Elder Watson and get him up here," I said with fake bravado. "We're not doing anything wrong."

Stalking off, the cook went in search of Elder Watson, the school principal. I tried to quell the tremor threatening to convulse my body. The shock in the room broken, students whispered among themselves while we waited. Girls shot looks of envy at me. My boys secretly applauded my display of wild machismo. Everybody expected me to be expelled.

I wasn't sure what was going to happen to me. But since I was already in deep, I was determined to enjoy my reason for sitting there. I fastened my eyes on Eloise, and began a casual conversation. Talking, laughing, and smiling as though this was just another ordinary day in the cafeteria. I could tell she was nervous. As the seconds ticked by, the small tremor I felt turned my insides to Jell-O.

Not more than three or four minutes passed before Elder Watson rushed into the dining room with Lefty hot on his heels. He beelined his way straight to our table, planting his full authority at my side. The room fell silent.

"Clifford. You know the rule."

"Yes sir," I said with respectful humbleness. "But I don't think there's anything wrong with what I'm doing, do you? I mean, do you think it's wrong for us to just sit and talk while we eat? I don't understand why boys and girls can't sit together and just talk."

"Because—it's the rule."

"But you can change the rule, can't you? You're the principal."

I was emboldened by Elder Watson's silence as he pondered the truth of my words. Since he hadn't expelled me immediately, I moved the spotlight from my blatant disobedience and changed the subject.

"And there's something else. I don't like the meals here and neither does anyone else."

"What's wrong with the food?" Elder Watson looked surprised and Lefty looked disgusted. I continued, with growing self-assuredness.

"It's the same thing, week after week. We know what we're going to eat before we come here. In the mornings," I threw a look at Lefty, "she makes pancakes with corn and string beans in them. Every Sabbath, we have apple pie and choplets."

Choplets are a meat substitute, made from soy and gluten, and are supposed to taste like beef. Having eaten real beef, the flavor of choplets didn't even come close. I hated the stuff.

Elder Watson listened patiently and quietly. It was eerie, how calm he had been through the whole episode. I didn't know what to make of it. I waited for his response.

"I understand what you've said and I promise I'll think about it, Clifford. All of it. In the meantime, I want you to move to the boys' side of the dining room."

No problem! I felt no need to argue and press my luck. I had respectfully made my point. So, I just picked up my tray and moved. And to my amazement, and everyone else's, I didn't get expelled. I wasn't even punished.

About a week later, the announcement came that boys and girls could sit together during meal times. True love had fought the battle and won. Elder Watson became my all-time favorite principal.

————•————

Because Pine Forge was secluded from the cities and towns close by, recreation and entertainment consisted of whatever the students thought of to do. Sports, games and weekend socials were the norm, but every once in a while something a little more exciting was needed.

My victory with Elder Watson cemented my reputation as a fearless rebel, in the eyes of my peers. But instead of using my leadership skills to do positive things, I did what any bored teenager who is hundreds of miles from home, and believes in his own invincibility against Elder Watson, would do. I led my crew in mischievous fun.

I never lost my childhood penchant for pranks and Pine Forge was ripe with opportunity. Sitting around with my three roommates on one of those boring nights, I had an idea.

"Hey, I've got a great idea." A wide grin covered my face. My roomies waited in anticipation for what I was going to say. "Let's sneak into the girls' dorm."

"What? Are you crazy?" they reeled back, shocked.

"Come on nobody's gonna see us," I continued. "It's dark and the deans are too busy with other stuff. We're not going to do anything. We're just going to say hello. It'll be fun."

Two of my three roommates didn't buy into my cavalier attitude.

"Clifford, if anyone saw us we'd be expelled right on the spot. I don't think it's a chance we should take."

Sucking my teeth, I rolled my eyes. The other roomie spoke before I could respond.

"Like Cliff said, who's gonna see us? We just make sure it's late enough that no one's around. It'll be great."

The two hold-outs were showing cracks, but weren't caving. They were still skeptical.

"Well, how we gonna get in?"

I shrugged my shoulders. "Easy. We'll use the vines on the side of the building to climb up the wall and go in through a window."

There was no question about a window being open. During nice weather, everybody kept their windows open since there were no air conditioners.

The hold-outs were weakening. I played my trump.

"We'll probably be the only guys to have ever gotten in."

I challenged their masochistic courageousness. If we pulled this off, our names would go down in the history books of swashbuckling, daredevil rule-breakers. Going to the girls' dorm had nothing to do with sex. It had everything to do with sneaking and not getting caught. The cracks busted wide open and the hold-outs broke.

"Okay. We're in."

"Yessss!" My comrade and I slapped hands.

Right before curfew, we left the dorm and stealthily made our way across campus through the darkness. I led the fearless three to the vines growing on the backside of the building. Stopping to catch our breath we rehearsed the plan.

"Okay," I whispered. "We climb the vines, one at a time, and go through that window." I pointed to the window above me.

Funny how nobody was concerned whether or not those vines would hold our solid, 15-year-old adolescent bodies. If anyone was worried, nothing was said. I went up first.

"Hello girls."

Somebody let out a small yelp and I threw my finger to my mouth with a shushing sound. I helped the other guys through the window. The girls calmed down and giggled while we strutted up and down the hall. None of them seemed angry or offended.

We had a few minutes of clean fun, then we cordially said our good-byes before high-tailing it back to our side of the campus to make curfew. Back in our room, we basked in our conquest, getting huge laughs from "our little secret."

We pulled this prank a few more times, never getting caught during the process. Imagine our shocked surprise the day my roommates and I received a summons to Elder Watson's office.

"Let me share with you," Elder Watson began in a tone void of hysteria, void of anger, void of any emotion, "why you gentlemen have been called here. It has come to my attention that you have been sneaking into the girls' dorm, at night. Is this true?"

Panic rose in my throat. My roommates looked like they would wet their pants. As the leader, I felt obligated to be the spokesperson, volunteering to take the blame.

"We only did it a few times, sir. It was a little joke."

"I don't care how many times you did it, it was wrong; and it is not a joke. And Clifford, since you are so quick to speak up I can safely assume that you are the ringleader?"

I didn't have to answer. Elder Watson's tone implied he already knew. He paced in front of us, talking directly into our faces.

"This is a Christian school where there are rules that must be obeyed. You all know what you did was wrong. You have admitted to violating the rules. This is behavior that I cannot, and will not tolerate from any student who attends this institution."

The punishment for our crime became clear when Elder Watson picked up the large wooden paddle he kept in his office. Sweat beads glistened on my forehead. Elder Watson beckoned to one of my roommates first. Disbelieving that the principal truly intended to whip a 15-year-old, my roommate shook his head.

"I'm sorry sir, but I'm not taking the whipping," my roommate respectfully objected. "I'll take any other punishment you give me, but that."

"You will take the paddling, or you will be expelled." Elder Watson was firm and final. He tapped his left palm with the wood, waiting for my roommate's decision. I stared at both of them. Elder Watson didn't budge. Just kept tapping the wood against his hand.

"Come on, we did wrong," I hissed somewhat under my breath. "We deserve it. So just take it and shut up!" I didn't care what the punishment was. I didn't want to leave Pine Forge.

My roommate couldn't bring himself to walk forward and bend over. Elder Watson tapped and waited.

"It's nothing," our other roommate hissed out of the side of his mouth. "It'll be over in a few minutes."

"Yeah," I chimed in. "It won't hurt much."

Elder Watson tapped and waited.

A look of humiliation swept across my roommate's face. I understood. It wasn't so much the paddling as it was getting whipped at our age and size that got to everybody. We saw ourselves as men. And here we were reduced to children. But there was no way around it unless we wanted to leave school. And nobody did. My roommate bent over, and our punishment commenced.

Needless to say, from then on our search for excitement did not involve breaking school rules. I learned my lesson, and it kept me in line for the rest of the year.

The school term flew by and before I knew it, it was time to go home for the summer. Pine Forge hadn't been so bad, after all. I had found love with Eloise and formed scores of friendships in a place where I had not wanted to go. I left Pine Forge looking forward to the next school year; looking forward to "picking up where I'd left off" with friends I would miss for the next two or three months.

I didn't know, then, that I would never again walk the Pine Forge campus as a student.

— — — — • — — — —

Work for my father had dried up in Oberlin during my year at Pine Forge. There wasn't enough business to keep all the brick masons working full-time. When I returned to Ohio for the summer, daddy told me he was moving the family again. This time, to Denver.

"Denver will provide me with more business opportunities," Daddy explained. "People there like their homes built with brick. And it will be good for you, with family living there." My mother's sister and her husband lived in Denver. It always seemed important for us to be around family.

I didn't want to move. I liked living in Oberlin. Our family was well known because of daddy's work and I had made lots of friends I didn't want to lose. It seemed every time I settled in a new place or new surroundings, I had to leave.

"I'll be able to go back to Pine Forge for school in the fall, right?"

Daddy shook his head. "I'm sorry Clifford, no. There's an Adventist high school in Denver you can attend.

I panicked. Moving meant leaving Eloise—a thought that made me want to vomit. Eloise lived in Philadelphia and being separated from her, even just for the summer, was tough to handle. Moving to Denver was like moving to the other side of the world. I'd never see her again! I had to convince my father to let me return to Pine Forge.

"Daddy, come on, please," I pleaded. "I'll come home to Denver for the summers."

"The entire family is moving to Denver, Clifford, and that includes you. You can go to school there."

I didn't want to go to Denver's academy. I wanted to go be with my friends. With Eloise. But Daddy's mind was made up. I knew by now that once he set his mind, he didn't change it. But I couldn't give in. My heart was at stake, so I tried reverse psychology.

"I didn't want to go to Pine Forge in the first place and you made me go. It was your idea, and it turned out to be a good one. Now that I want to stay, you're forcing me to leave. Why are you doing this? Why are you insisting that I move too? There are good families I know I could stay with during holidays. People you know and respect. Come on, dad..."

No matter what scheme I devised, it wasn't good enough. My father's final, firm response was "You belong with us."

I was devastated. Pine Forge had given me so much. It gave me independence by forcing me to live away from home. I'd found acceptance among my peers. I'd found love with Eloise. The thought of leaving her was the most crushing blow.

From that moment on, there was nothing joyful about that summer. Mama went to Denver ahead of daddy and me. We were staying behind to go to camp meeting; an annual ten-day retreat where Adventists gather for spiritual renewal. Daddy sacrificed to stay behind and take me to Pine Forge's camp-meeting for the weekend so I could say good-bye to Eloise.

I was somber as daddy and I rode the 400 mile trip from Oberlin to Pine Forge, even though we rode in style. Daddy had just purchased a brand new Oldsmobile 98. It boosted my spirits a little when daddy let me get behind the wheel and drive part of the way, testing out my brand new driver's license.

Campmeeting was bittersweet. Eloise and I spent most of our time walking and talking. I rarely left her side. I used that weekend to memorize everything about her; her look, her smell, her voice, her smile. If I couldn't physically be with her, I would inhale her into my soul and take her memory with me when I moved.

"You will always be my girl, Eloise," I fervently promised. I gave my word to be true to her; not like other guys who had girlfriends but would date others on the side. I was determined to be the kind of man daddy taught me to be—the kind that stayed faithful to his woman and did not run around. We also promised to write each other faithfully, every week.

When campmeeting ended, we drove Eloise and her mother home to Philadelphia. It was 50 miles from the campground and daddy let me drive. At 16, sitting behind the wheel of a new car with my woman beside me, I felt larger than life. It didn't matter that Eloise was sandwiched between me and daddy, nor that her mother sat in the back seat. In my mind we were the only two people in the car.

As she closed the car door and walked away toward her house, thick darkness filled my chest. I swallowed hard, trying to force my throat open as it closed in on me. Subconsciously, maybe I knew that this was the end. The void I felt, I would much later try to fill, though miserably failing to do so.

After a few weeks, daddy and I left Oberlin and moved to Denver. Loneliness came with me.

It was June, 1956.

— — — — •— — — —

In the fall, I entered Denver Academy as a student. Denver Academy was an Adventist day school, predominately attended by White students. On my first day, I was shocked to discover that it was ONLY attended by White students, until I came. I was the sole Black student in the entire school.

Immediately I felt out of place. Coming from an all-Black school where I had a bonded sense of identity with fellow students, to an all-White school where my identity was conspicuously separate from everyone else's, required a major adjustment. I was in a glaring spotlight, and I felt uncomfortable. It must not have showed, though, because I got along well with all the students. I never had problems with any of them.

My problems were with the grown-ups.

I never felt accepted by any of my teachers, particularly my English teacher. She despised my very existence in her class. Almost every day she singled me out with some negative remark. Whether she fussed or belittled me, her tone of voice always "kept me in my place," beneath everyone else in the class.

I was no stranger to prejudice. I grew up in the south where Blacks encountered prejudice everywhere. I remember the time, while still a little boy, the police almost lynched my brother Melvin. He accidentally hit a policeman's car, and they took him to jail and beat him. After getting Melvin out of jail— a small miracle in itself—my parents sent him north to live with relatives.

I remember traveling through the south and using separate water fountains and restrooms at gas stations. I was completely aware of the country's feelings toward Blacks. Maybe I just hadn't expected the same treatment from so-called Christians.

Already a below-average student, my work didn't improve. The prejudice I encountered from my teachers made me hate school. Slowly, the bad taste in my mouth turned into a bad attitude. Had it not been for the students, I would have exploded long before I did.

I was one of five boys in my class. Four of us developed a strong friendship, becoming very close. Chuck, Ronnie, Doug and I were constantly hanging together, in and out of school. Their parents were my parents and my parents were their parents, as we often spent the night at each other's homes. The color lines between us melted as fast as Denver snow in the hot sun.

I was particularly close with Chuck. Out of the four, I considered him my best friend. Chuck was a huge guy, very brawny and handsome. The girls at school always showered Chuck with attention. Though very popular, Chuck wasn't arrogant or conceited. And my blackness didn't phase him at all. Not caring what anyone else thought about our friendship, he never hesitated to include me in anything that went on in school. His acceptance of me made it easier for other students to accept me.

But the adults in the school continued making my life hell.

Prom night was coming. Students excitedly made plans about who was asking who, and who was wearing what.

"I would like to remind you," said the principal, "that students at Denver Academy are not allowed to bring outside students to the prom. You can only bring someone who attends this school."

Fastening his eyes on me, he continued. "But for you, Clifford, we'll make an exception. You can bring someone from outside."

Maybe the principal expected me to feel privileged that he was breaking school policy for me. I guess I should have jumped up and down, clapping my hands and bobbing my head, saying "Thankya sah. I's really do appreciate you doin' that for me, sah." Instead, I fixed him with a cool gaze, as heat crept up my face.

"Why are you making a special exception for me?"

The principal turned beet red. He cleared his throat. He looked ill. He cleared his throat, again. I stared unflinchingly into his eyes, waiting for an answer to my question hanging in the air like thick smoke.

Don't get me wrong. I was no more interested in taking a White girl to the prom than he was afraid of me asking one.

But I wanted him to know that I wasn't stupid. His attempt to veil his prejudice as a show of good will was thin, and I wasn't buying it. I was sick of the discriminatory attitudes displayed by the school's faculty and staff.

When the principal found his voice, he stammered out some answer I can't even remember. Obviously it wasn't a revelation. But my point was made. Without another word, I turned and walked away.

I decided not to go to the prom, but Chuck, Ronnie and Doug weren't having it.

"Aw come on Clifford," they begged me. "You've gotta go to the prom. It's the biggest event we have, and we're not going without you. Don't let these people get to you. They're the ones with a problem, not us. Come on. You know we'll have fun."

After their incessant pestering, I finally agreed to go. I asked a girl from my church, Eddie Jean, to go as my date. Just a friend date, though, because my true love was still Eloise. I was still writing letters to her, affirming my love and faithfulness, although her letters were coming a little more infrequently.

We had a good time at the prom, though my full heart wasn't in it. I felt a little guilty going out with Eddie Jean even though we were just friends. I lived and breathed Eloise. And I didn't want to do anything to jeopardize our love for each other.

After the prom, nothing at school changed. The vicious cycle of negative attitudes continued—the discrimination from the teachers and my increasingly negative behavior toward them. I longed for the days at Pine Forge where I was accepted by everyone. I longed for Eloise.

One day a piece of mail was waiting for me when I got home from school. It was a letter from Eloise. Finally!! I was so excited. The butterflies in my stomach fluttered around, making me queasy with anticipation. I opened the letter and began reading. As my eyes floated over each line, the queasiness turned to nausea. What I was holding wasn't a letter of love. It was a "Dear John" letter. Eloise had another boyfriend. She was breaking up with me.

I couldn't believe it. Here I had been true to her all these years; turning away girls who'd been interested in me, never having eyes for anyone else. And I get a "Dear John" letter? Why didn't she just literally pull my heart out of my chest and stomp on it? She was divorcing me.

If I were thinking sensibly, I couldn't blame her. I mean, four years of letters and never seeing or talking to each other is not the way to nurture a relationship. But who was thinking sensibly?

I was devastated. And to make matters worse, I didn't have anyone to talk to about it. I couldn't talk to mama or daddy. I couldn't talk to Chuck or Ronnie, or Doug. Nobody could understand how I was feeling. No one could fathom the pain I felt having my devotion to Eloise cruelly ripped apart.

All I had was that letter and those words piercing me over and over again. I wallowed in a miserable stupor. Denver had ruined my life. It took away my self esteem. It took away my friends. And it took away the girl I was supposed to marry.

My attitude at school got worse, if that was possible. Finally, I couldn't take it anymore.

"I'm leaving school," I told the guys one day.

"What do you mean? Are you going somewhere else?"

"No. I'm quitting."

Each guy took his turn begging me to stay. But I couldn't stomach the constant turmoil I felt. I was always used as the class example of bad school work, stupid mistakes, inferior learning abilities. The teachers relentlessly battered my already low self-esteem. Even my close friendship with Chuck, Ronnie and Doug couldn't replace what they chipped away. To save what little esteem I had left, I had to get out.

So I quit.

— — — • — — —

I kept in touch with the guys; still hanging out when we could. But I was working now. Making money. And my feelings of manhood began to change the dynamics of our friendship. As far as I was concerned they were boys, still in school. I was standing on the brink of manhood, making my own way. Every so often they tried to convince me to come back to school. But I didn't belong there and refused to return.

One day I arrived home from work to find my mother in a solemn mood.

"Clifford, I have some bad news." Mama's face poured out concern and hurt. My mind raced as I tried to predict what she was about to say.

"What, mama?"

"Chuck;" she searched for the most gentle, sensitive words to use but there were none. "Chuck, is dead."

My blood ran cold. I felt what seemed to be a lightening bolt sear through my body, something fierce enough to knock me out of my shoes to the other side of the room. My head felt light as reality became a dream, a nightmare of words trying to bore their way into my consciousness.

"You're lying," I choked out. "YOU'RE LYING. THAT CAN'T BE TRUE."

Tears coursed down my cheeks. I refused to make sense out of mama's words.

"I'm sorry Clifford. It is true, and I'm so sorry." Mama gave me the details.

It was September, 1957. The new school year was a few weeks into term. Chuck, Ronnie and Doug had gone hiking in the mountains. They discovered an abandoned mine and were playing around. I can imagine their giddy delight at the discovery, and the daring, bold attitude teenage boys so often experience when they're on an adventure. A boldness that pushes the boundaries of good sense.

Chuck fell into one of the mine shafts—his life snuffed out. My best friend, gone. His encouraging voice, silenced. His open acceptance, closed. I could not reject the truth any longer. Chuck was dead. I felt vacant.

Chuck's mom asked me to be a pallbearer at his funeral. That she considered this Black kid special enough to Chuck and his family to give me a place of honor in a sea of White faces, filled me with gratitude. It was the ultimate gesture of acceptance. And the ultimate feeling of pain.

Chuck's mom approached me after the funeral. Putting a comforting hand on my arm, she looked into my face. Kindly, she said, "Clifford, Chuck had a lot of respect for you as a person and a friend. He felt disappointed when you quit school, because he knew you had what it took to hang in there. It bothered him, how you were treated, but he wished you hadn't let it push you out. He often talked about how he wanted you to come back and finish."

I knew what was coming next. How could I say no? If I wouldn't go back to school for myself, maybe I could go back to honor my best friend's wish. The sensible part of me knew nothing at school had changed. Besides, I enjoyed the money I was making as a bricklayer. Giving that up was hard to consider. But the loyal part of me knew there was nothing I wouldn't give up in honor of Chuck's friendship. So, I went back to school.

I knew I made a mistake the first day I stepped my foot back into that same English teacher's classroom. She must have missed me something awful. She had no one to denigrate or humiliate when I wasn't there. She showed me how much she'd missed my Black face by picking up right where she'd left off. If her mistreatment was hard to take the year before, it was harder now. I had changed. I considered myself a man. A working man, at that. I was probably making more money than any of the faculty and staff in the school.

One day, she taunted and criticized me one time too many. The anger boiled over, furiously erupting from my gut. I shot out of my desk chair, fighting to control the urge to get up in her face.

"I AM SICK AND TIRED OF YOUR S— LADY! You prance around here like you're somebody IMPORTANT just because you're WHITE! SO WHAT. YOU'RE WHITE. BUT YOU AIN'T NOTHING! YOU HEAR ME? NOTHING! You ain't a good Christian and you ain't even a good teacher. In fact, YOU are the WORST teacher I have EVER had."

I was breathing hard, heavy and fast, my face contorted with rage. Angry English, the improper kind that spills out in fury, was venom to her ears. As far as I knew and cared, it was just me and her in that classroom. Her steely blue eyes smiled in triumph. I had confirmed her stereotypical definition of my kind.

"You go to the principal's office RIGHT NOW!" Her voice was icy.

I snatched up my books and marched to the principal's office, determined to get justice. As I explained why I was there I watched the walls close around him. I might as well have been bouncing ping pong balls off his head. He completely tuned me out.

"You were wrong Mr. Harris," he said when I finished my spill.

"Me? ME? What do you mean, I was wrong?"

"You disrespected a teacher. And you did it in front of her class."

"AND? She disrespected ME in front of my class!"

"I am not interested in what you say she did."

"Excuse me? In what I *say* she did. What? You sayin', I'm lyin? Obviously, you don't understand what's been happening! I'm telling you, this teacher has singled me out from day one, and..." The principal interrupted me.

"YOU are the one who misbehaved Mr. Harris, and I will not tolerate any student disrespecting a teacher in this school." BAM! He slammed his mind's door shut, right in my face.

I about lost my mind. I fired up his white ears, turning them red hot with filthy street language we Adventist kids knew, but never unleashed in our Christian circles. Especially on adults.

"You're just like her, you little piece of s—! You think you better too, because of your WHITENESS?"

I watched the principal's neck veins pop up and begin to throb. Redness slowly enveloped his entire head.

"Well, let me tell you somethin'. I can go out and work hourly, and make more money than you ever will in this school. All ya'll prejudiced as hell. Ain't none of you worth nothin'. I'm outta this hell hole!"

I whooshed out of the building as if riding a strong wind. I jumped in my car, started it up, and drove in circles in front of the school. Faster and faster I drove, spinning the wheels, round and round, churning up the dirt. Mixing it with all of my pent-up frustration and anger—leaving Pine Forge, being dumped by Eloise, discrimination, Chuck's death.

I knew all the White people in that school were not prejudiced. But the attitudes of those who were conjured up old feelings I was always trying to run down. Feeling different.
Feeling inferior. Feeling isolated. Feeling bad. I was sick of it.

I sped out of the parking lot that day, leaving my school
days and all educational pursuits behind. For good.

Be *happy, young man, while you are*
young, and let your heart give you joy
in the days of your youth.
Follow the ways of your heart
and whatever your eyes see, but know that
for all these things
God will bring you to judgment.
Ecclesiastes 11:9

Chapter 4

ON THE BRINK

had no trouble finding work. I got a job as a mason's helper, and I laid brick on the side for some extra money. Quitting school was no big deal. It wasn't doing me any good anyway. I wasn't learning anything I needed to know to survive. At 17, I felt I knew everything I needed to know. I proved that after quitting school the first time—when I bought my first car.

When I told daddy I wanted to buy a car, he was eagerly supportive. Particularly as he told me I'd have to earn the money myself. But that was okay. I'd already been saving money.

I dreamed about my car all the time. I knew just what I wanted. A 1950, ebony black, four-door Ford. Everywhere I went my eyes were peeled for my dream car. Not one car lot in Denver escaped my scrutiny, which finally paid off on a Friday afternoon. I saw my car on a lot on Colfax Avenue.

"That's it!" I tingled with excitement. I couldn't believe I was actually looking at the car of my dreams—a four-door sedan with gray interior and cloth seats. Uncontained, I went straight to daddy's job, unable to wait until evening when I'd see him at home.

"Ah, you've got to see it, dad, man. It's beautiful." I gushed, describing every minute detail while thinking in the back of my mind that daddy probably didn't care about the car that much. But he listened intently while I buzzed on and on, finally ending again with "you've just got to see it."

"Well let's go see it." Daddy began putting away his tools.

Excuse me? Who is this man? This couldn't be MY father, the one I'd always heard say "a bricklayer doesn't walk off the job." This couldn't be the man who stayed on a job, once he started, until he finished or it got too dark to see anymore. Yet—here he was, putting away his tools, willing to quit work two hours early just so he could go with me to look at a car. Daddy's simple gesture that day meant the world to me.

It was tough trying to be cool as we neared the car lot. My excitement gurgled just beneath my exterior. Standing by the car, I gazed on it adoringly, lovingly stroking the black finish. I was in love, again, but not with a woman—but with a fine piece of machinery. Daddy didn't say much as I extolled all its wonderful virtues, though he agreed it was in good condition for its age. The salesman came over to talk.

"My son, here, likes this car. How much is it?" Daddy and the salesman talked back and forth. I listened as they each took their bargaining turn. When daddy was satisfied, he co-signed a loan for me to buy the car. It was a manly moment when I counted off $500 of MY money as a down payment for MY car. Life had just gotten great.

I drove my black beauty off the lot, feeling like a full-grown man. Life was changing, and I was on the brink of stepping into a whole new era. As the perfect, finishing touch to my new love, I had the words "Black Satin" painted in silver sprawling script on the bottom of the left and right sides of the front fenders. Some jazz group had cut an album by that name. When I heard it—Black Satin— it so eloquently described how the car looked in my eyes that I adopted the name.

My love affair with Black Satin was in full bloom.

————•————

Without school, and Chuck, I lost my circle of friends. I had nothing in common with the kids at church who were my age. And I didn't see them as being fun people. Needing a group to hang out with, I began running around with kids from Manual High, a large public school where most of the students were Black and Hispanic. My two main buddies were *Lennie Gaines and *Rick Owens.

Lennie and Rick were a couple of years younger than me. Lennie was very tall for his age and a guy who loved to look good—always dressed clean and sharp. Rick was short and fearless. He didn't take anything off of anybody, and it took very little to get his temper riled up.

Their first attraction to me was my car. Having my own transportation, and always having money, made me cool to be around. They had no problem using me for my resources, but I didn't mind. I just wanted to be accepted. That's what they gave me in return—along with some great times.

Lennie, the leader of our group, always came up with stuff to do. Little did I know how much of an impact he would have on my life for many years to come. Hanging out one day, I saw Lennie and Rick animatedly talking about something.

"What's all the excitement about?" I asked.

"Yo man, a bunch of us is going to the Little Richard concert Friday night," Lennie replied. "You comin'?"

I was thrown into immediate conflict. Friday night, the beginning of Sabbath, I was expected to go to church like most of the Adventist teens did. Going to a rock concert on Friday night would be breaking the Sabbath. Besides, my parents wouldn't allow me to go to a rock concert if it was on "Anyday" night. They considered rock-n-roll sinful music, and since I was living in their house under their rules, they'd forbid me to go.

"I don't know man. I'm not sure if I'm free."

*Names have been changed.

51

"Aw man! Whatchu got to do?"

No way was I telling Lennie about church and my parents' rules. I'd look like a sissy. Besides, I hated their rules, and Friday night choir rehearsals bored me to death. I considered the teens at church children because they were still in school, while I was a working man with my own car. And as a man, I had a right to do what I wanted to do.

"Ain't nothin' deep, man," I casually replied, shrugging my shoulders. "I'll letcha know if I'm goin'. I probably will."

I didn't quite feel man enough to out and out defy my parents. I wouldn't have won and I didn't need the headache anyway. So I decided to lie without lying.

"Mama, daddy, I'm going to church," I said heading out the door Friday night. And I did go to church, just staying a few minutes. Then I met Lennie and my other friends at the Little Richard concert and had an absolute blast.

Oh yeah—of course I had twinges of guilt. After all, I was consciously breaking the most sacred, respected hours of the week. I was going directly against the only values I'd ever been taught. But feeling accepted by the "in" crowd and doing what I wanted to do were more important to me now. And make no mistake about it—this was fun!

The value of honesty so ingrained in me, began degenerating into sneaky half-truths. The Friday night pattern never changed. "Where are you going?" my mother would ask. "To church," I'd reply. "We're having choir practice." And I'd go to choir practice for about 20 minutes, then meet my buddies wherever the evening's activities took place. Each lie sliced a little piece of my self worth away without my even noticing.

Lennie opened up a whole new world to me and I soaked it up like a newborn baby. Canteens—what would be considered dance clubs now— were popular hang outs then. The music blasting and people dancing and just hanging out was the wildest scene I'd ever experienced.

I couldn't dance worth a lick, but I sure tried. Arms and feet going different directions, no rhythm. I didn't care. Just the mere freedom and abandonment I felt, made me feel great. The more I danced, the better I got. I even learned how to slow dance. I'd wrap my arms around a girl and pull her real close, feeling our bodies melt together, swaying together, creating furious heat. I'd close my eyes and see Eloise's face snuggled under my chin; feel her body swaying with mine. Even after our breakup, my heart was still with her.

THIS was the life! I felt totally accepted by my new crowd, a feeling that felt better than good. They laughed at my jokes, egged my no-dancing self on, and made me feel I was one of them.

But to my parents, I was still one of THEM. The church-going, choir-singing Christian young man with the same morals and values they'd raised me with. For a while, they didn't know I was leading a double life. They had no idea what I was doing on Friday nights, or if they did, they never let on.

As an Adventist, I knew what I was doing was wrong. But at 17 and 18, all I cared about was having fun. With my friends, I didn't have to hear how bad I was, or how much I was sinning. Nobody was looking down on me, shaking their finger in my face and talking about where I was going because of my sinful ways. They didn't have to. My conscience screamed loud enough. To quiet that insistent voice, I rationalized by telling myself I wasn't giving up EVERYTHING I'd been taught.

"Hey. Put that cigarette out," I'd emphatically say to Lennie and whoever else was riding in Black Satin.

"No smoking or drinking in my car. I ain't into that."

And I wasn't. I may have been hanging out with them, but I wasn't living like them. I did draw a line. And so did mama and daddy.

As long as I lived under their roof, there were rules to obey. They insisted on treating me like a 10-year-old. Every time I got ready to leave the house they asked; "Where are you going? What time will you be back?" As a man, I didn't think I should have to tell them my business or abide by their ridiculous rules. Obviously, they didn't share my view.

"Clifford," daddy said, "you're going to be inside this house by twelve o'clock at night." Not, "I would like you to be," but "you're going to be," said with his there's-no-discussion voice.

I obeyed. And I hated it. There was nothing more deflating than to be driving home to my unyielding parents and their rules after hanging out with Lennie, doing what I wanted. "It's time to go," I started saying to myself. "I have got to move out and get my own place. They're really cramping my style."

Besides, I wanted to be on my own—fend for myself. I needed to take away the cushion of having my food and shelter sure, living with mama and daddy. I needed to become a man. That was the only way I could carry out my real plan—going back to Philadelphia to fight for Eloise. Getting her to marry me. All I had to do was figure out how to get daddy to agree to let me move out.

One day I got a break. Or so I thought.

"I'm heading to New Mexico for a while," daddy informed me. Work had gotten real slow in Denver, and Albuquerque offered a good job opportunity for him. What that meant to me, though, was the iron fist wouldn't be around to police my midnight curfew. I tried to hold back my glee.

Heading out the door one night, mama stopped my hang-out plans, cold.

"Clifford, just because your father's not here, don't think you can come home whenever you want to. You still got a curfew, and I expect you to be back in this house by twelve o'clock EVERY night. Understand?" Mama's face was dead serious.

"Aw come on mama..." I started, but she checked me.

"No, I ain't playing. If you're not home by twelve o'clock, you won't be coming in THIS house because the door WILL BE locked." Her face changed from serious to a hand on the hip, neck-rolling, "you-go-on-and-try-me" face. I wasn't stupid. And I wasn't disrespectful. I begrudgingly obeyed, hating every minute.

Two or three nights later I left the house to hang out with Lennie and the fellas. Acting crazy in downtown Denver, drag racing, laughing, talking and singing, I'd unintentionally lost track of time. I drove up to my house a little after 12:30 p.m.

Everything was dark and quiet. I pulled Black Satin into the garage, then walked to the back door. I turned the handle. It didn't budge. I tried it again. Nothing. *Nah*, I thought, kind of chuckling to myself, *Mama didn't lock me out. She just locked this door without thinking.*

I went around to the front door. I turned the handle. Locked! My mind went on instant rewind and that serious conversation replayed in my head. "If you're not home by twelve o'clock," I saw mama saying, "you won't be coming in THIS house because the door WILL BE locked."

And don't you know, she actually did it. She locked me out. I stood there. Stunned. For a few seconds I wasn't sure what to do.

Slowly I walked back to the garage, opened up Black Satin's door, got in, and sat there. In the car. With realization dawning on me that I'd be spending the night in my car. I tried to make myself comfortable, but there was no way to really be comfortable.

As the night wore on, the frigid air wore me out. With no blankets and no heat, I sat in my car, my body wracked with a bone-piercing chill that didn't permit me to really sleep. I cat napped.

At the first glimmer of dawn I wanted to check the doors, but I forced myself to wait until I knew mama was up. Then, I walked to the back door warily reaching out to grab the handle. It turned.

I stepped into the house. Mama stood at the stove cooking breakfast. As she heard me step in, she threw a glance at me, our eyes locking for an instant. She turned away saying nothing. She didn't have to. She had won. I was steaming mad. But the next night, and every night thereafter, I was home by curfew.

As my parents and I continued to clash, the friction got harder and harder to bear. My desire for Eloise grew stronger and stronger. Not a day went by that I didn't contemplate leaving home for good.

It is better to heed a wise man's rebuke
than to listen to the song
of fools.
Proverbs 7:5

Chapter 5

LIFE CHANGES

The more I hung out with Lennie, Rick and the rest of the Manual High crowd, the more I changed. Their influence pulled me further and further away from my Christian core. I bought into their I-don't-give-a-care, I-can-do-whatever-I-want attitude as freedom, and wore it like a badge when out of my parents' sight.

I was 19. Black Satin and I had been together for over a year and she needed a little face lift. It was 1959, and the hot car thing was dummy spotlights. A lot of guys put little dummy spotlights on their cars. It was a cool look, and I didn't want to be left out. I wanted a set of lights really bad.

I couldn't afford to buy a set and it was out of the question to ask my parents for the money. But I had to have those lights. Every time I saw a car go by with dummy spotlights, my need to have them grew stronger and stronger. Always wanting to belong, I ached to have a pair to put on Black Satin.

Racking my brain for a way to get some of those lights, an idea hit me. The airport! The parking lot was always filled with cars, one of which, I knew, would have those lights. I could easily steal a pair, because no one surveyed the parking lot 24 hours a day. Or so I thought.

I hadn't stolen anything since the money I'd taken as a child from daddy. I don't remember whether I had any reservations about stealing again. All I know is the power of wanting to fit in eclipsed any good impulses.

I drove to the airport, slowly casing cars in the parking lot. When I spotted a car with dummy lights, I parked. Grabbing my screw driver, I nonchalantly walked to the car, glancing around to make sure no one stood nearby. Completely engrossed in what I was doing, trying to do it quickly, I didn't hear or see anyone walk up behind me.

"What are you doing?"

The voice startled me and I swirled around to face it. There stood a White man in plain clothes, looking at me very intently. Trapped, my brain moved fast trying to decide what to do.

"I...a...," I couldn't even get any words out. In a flash, the man morphed into a pit bull.

"Turn around and put your hands behind your back," he snarled at me. He slammed me down on the car. I felt cold steel dig into my flesh as he handcuffed my wrists.

"You're under arrest for attempted theft. You have the right..."

Fog clouded my brain and the sound of blood rushing through my body drowned out the man's words. Sweat beads dotted my forehead. The policeman pushed me into the back seat of his car and drove away.

At the county jail, I was a routine process. Cops filled out paperwork with my name on it. They pressed my fingers into the ink and rolled them onto the paper, leaving me indelibly marked. Camera light flashed in my eyes as they photographed my face, forever linked with the numbers I held up.

I dialed my one phone call to my father at home, scared and dreading what I had to say.

"Daddy (long pause) I need you to come get me."

"Why? Where's your car?"

"At the airport."

"Where are you?"

I had the hardest time getting the words out. My mind carried me back to my childhood, standing in front of daddy when he asked me where his money was.

"At the county jail," I spat out.

The silence pulsated. That awful, heavy silence you can cut with a knife. No more questions. No more answers. Just silence. Then...

"I'll be right there."

I hung up the phone. As I waited, my thoughts beat me over the head; *What is wrong with you?* My mind screamed; *"How could you be so dumb! Those lights aren't even worth going to jail for."* How I wished I could turn back time and start all over again. I played the "if only" game. If only I hadn't wanted those lights so bad. If only I hadn't gone to the airport. If only...

When daddy arrived, the police filled him in on the charges. Facing daddy, I was that 12-year-old kid again. Him looking at me with disappointment. Me looking at him with shame, nothing adequate to say.

I didn't have to stay in jail. Since I hadn't actually taken anything and I had no prior record, they released me to my father with an order to return for a court hearing a few days later.

I stood before the judge in court, daddy at my side. My outfit screamed "respectable citizen." After all, I really wasn't a criminal. I had just made a stupid, bad mistake.

"How do you plead?" the judge asked.

"Guilty." The words hung there for a minute.

"Since you have no prior record and you appear to be genuinely penitent, this court fines you $300 to be paid before you leave here today."

BANG! The gavel cracked the desk.

"WHAT DID HE SAY?" daddy asked in a loud voice as if he was hard of hearing. He'd heard perfectly well what the judge said.

"He said that would be $300," I repeated without looking at daddy.

"I ain't got $300."

"Well sir, if you don't have $300, your son will have to stay in jail until you can get $300."

"I'm sorry judge, but I ain't got it." My mouth flew open. I sucked in my breath.

"Then take him away," the judge responded coolly.

I wanted to cry. But at 19, my pride wouldn't let me cry. I stared at daddy incredulously. His jaw was tight, his body stiff. My own father had kicked me to the curb. His flesh and blood. His son. I felt utterly rejected. I wanted to beg him for forgiveness. Beg him to pay the fine. Beg him not to let them put me in jail. Plead that I had learned my lesson and that I'd be good from now on. But I knew it wouldn't make a difference.

Humiliated, I hung my head as the deputy led me from the courtroom. They took my clothes. They took my personal belongings. They took my real identity. To them, I was nothing but a no good criminal.

All that freedom I'd felt hanging with Lennie and my friends dissipated in one poof, as the cell bars clanged together shutting me off from my world. I was locked up in this foul-smelling, filthy square, unable to escape. I laid on the cot to dream away reality, lulled by the constant jail noise.

Two days passed before I heard my name on the loud speaker.

"Harris, wrap it up," the voice said, using prison jargon for "you are going home."

Excitement flickered inside my soul as I put on my own

clothes and took back my own identity. I stood at the desk waiting for my personal belongings, when daddy walked up beside me. I resisted the powerful urge to hug him.

"Clifford, are you going to pay me this money back?"

"Oh yeah daddy. You know I will." I was cavalier and half hearted in my response. I was more concerned with getting out of that place, than with the money my father would have to spend to get me out.

"No you ain't. You ain't going to pay me back." Daddy turned to the policeman. "Take him back and lock him up again."

He might as well have punched the wind out of me and kicked me in the groin. Not caring about whatever was going on between me and daddy, the policeman locked me up again.

I had two more days to think about what I had done to myself, and to my father. When I heard that loud speaker yell my name and I went through the release procedure again, I was scared as heck that daddy would renege. When he asked me if I was going to pay him back, I enthusiastically bobbed my head and *"yes sirred"* with every ounce of believability I could muster.

The fresh air and sunshine never felt so good as they did that day. Walking to the car daddy turned to me and said "You stole something Clifford. You had no business doing that. I'm sorry I left you in jail, but you're too big to whip and that was the only way I knew to teach you a lesson."

I understood that. Yes, I had felt hurt and rejected. But I wasn't angry. I understood perfectly where daddy was coming from.

I wish I could say that experience changed the direction I was headed in. But my head was too hard. My value system was shifting. That little voice I'd heard so loudly when I'd started going against my parents' teachings was getting more faint. My life was changing, yet I could barely perceive it. Neither could I recognize the lessons my changing lifestyle brought.

By the way, I never did pay daddy back the money.

— — — — • — — — —

Hanging with Lennie provided continuing education on how to live life outside the church, and I was a willing student. My no smoking, no drinking policy faded away as Lennie schooled me on how to live the good life.

"Whaddaya think? Ain't this stuff great?," Lennie asked me, smiling.

I tried not to screw my face up too much. But the aftertaste in my mouth was so bitter. "It's okay, I mean, it ain't all that, but it's alright."

"Aw man, you just got to get used to it, that's all."

Lennie threw his head back and chugged the wine from the bottle. His eyes squinched shut and he pursed his lips.

"Whoo boy," he hollered. He opened his eyes and smacked his lips. "Here," he said, handing the bottle back to me, "try some more."

I grabbed the bottle of Thunderbird, a red wine that all the brothers seemed to drink. Probably because it was so cheap— about 99 cents a quart. Drinking Thunderbird was like drinking gasoline, especially when compared to the more refined, expensive wines.

I'd never drank alcohol and I couldn't understand what the big deal was. But nobody partied or hung out without it. Everybody drank. So I'd decided to try it.

I took another swig, although I didn't really like the taste— real sweet with a biting bitterness. But the more I drank, the bigger the warm glow grew inside my body. A glow like you feel when the sun comes out in winter and bathes your body in heat. That's the only good feeling, because the alcohol's heat eventually tingled in a way that didn't feel good.

I drank the wine anyway. Mainly because my friends did and it wasn't harmful. Or so I thought. I may not have drank enough for alcohol to harm me physically, but I drank enough for it to harm me psychologically. It was breaking down my mental and moral resistance to experimenting with other substances.

I just didn't know it then.

———•———

It was summer time, and so far, I hadn't come up with any good plan for moving away from home and I was more than ready. I needed to be on my own, and I needed to get to Eloise to convince her that we were supposed to be together.

I racked my brain everyday, scheming for ways to get out of the house. Then it hit me. I could go to Melvin's. My brother Melvin, who had stayed in Oberlin with his wife, was making a good living working construction. If I lived with him, I would still have the security of food, shelter and a job, but I'd be more on my own than I was living with mama and daddy.

If I got to Oberlin, I knew I could get to Eloise with no problem. It was camp meeting time at Pine Forge, and a trip to Ohio right now would be perfect timing. If Eloise could see me and talk with me, she'd realize how much she still loved me and how we were destined to be together. Then we could get married, and life would be grand.

The trick was getting to Oberlin without daddy knowing my real plan. I decided to approach the trip as a summer work excursion. I'd just visit Melvin for the summer to work with him. Daddy did it all the time—going off to other towns where work was more plentiful. I'd be doing the same thing, something daddy would understand.

My plan still had kinks, though. In daddy's eyes I was young and inexperienced. I knew he wouldn't approve of me driving that long distance to Oberlin, alone. I needed someone to go with me. I thought of my baby sister.

"Sandra," I said with a sense of adventure in my voice, "how would you like to go visit Melvin?"

"What, by myself?"

"No, you and me, together." Sandra sort of shrugged her shoulders nonchalantly.

"How would we get there?"

"We'd drive. Black Satin. Just you and me. We'll go for the whole summer. I can work and you can just cool out. It'll give us a little break from home—a nice vacation. Whataya say?"

Sandra's agreement to ride with me completed my plan. I took it to daddy with confidence.

"Daddy, I think I'm going to drive to Oberlin and visit Melvin." I glanced at his face for a reaction. "I figured I could spend the summer working with him, making some good money. Sandra's gonna ride with me so I won't be driving by myself."

Apparently, I had thought through everything, cause daddy agreed to let me go. I was ecstatic. Everything came together like clock work.

Sandra and I set out in Black Satin headed for Ohio. I planned to spend a couple of days with Melvin, then leave Sandra with him and drive alone to campmeeting at Pine Forge. To win back Eloise.

Somewhere in Kansas my plan went haywire. Driving down the highway in the dark of night, I started hearing noises coming from the back of the car.

"What is that?" Sandra asked. The car was whining and thumping—making a huge racket. An inkling of what was happening toyed with my mind, but I didn't want to believe it. I kept on driving.

"Cliff, what's wrong with the car? Why is it making all that noise?" Sandra's voice was a little more urgent.

"I'm not sure," I replied, trying to sound calm. I could feel the rear wheels of the car beginning to lock up and just skid along instead of rotating. I pulled Black Satin over on the highway shoulder and jumped out to see what was wrong. I looked under the back of the car and my fears were confirmed.

"Aw crap!"

"WHAT?" Sandra asked.

"The rear end is going bad."

"What does that mean?"

"It means we have to get another one." I got back in the car and slammed the door shut. I knew I couldn't make it to Ohio, but I could make it to the closest town. I started the car and pulled back onto the road. Sandra threw a worried look at me.

"So what are we going to do?"

"We can't do anything until morning."

"WHAT? What do you mean we can't do anything?" Sandra was agitated.

"Just what I said. I can't fix the problem without parts. It's nighttime, Sandra. It's not like I can go anywhere and get parts now. Everything's closed. So we'll have to wait until morning."

The air in the car tensed with anger and worry. Once we got to the next town, I spotted an auto junkyard. I pulled the car over and we slept in the car, in front of the junkyard, waiting for it to open. The next morning, I found the parts I needed and I fixed Black Satin on the side of the road where we'd slept.

I spent so much money on parts to fix Black Satin, there

was no way to continue the trip. I swallowed my disappointment and we turned around heading back home. I had lost this round, but I wasn't down and out yet.

I worked hard for a week, putting in lots of overtime. I was on a mission. I saved my money with the soul of a miser, only buying bare necessities. I planned to try the trip again. Surprisingly, Sandra agreed to go with me.

Once again, we started for Ohio. This time we made it with no trouble. But I had missed Pine Forge's campmeeting. If I wanted to see Eloise I'd have to drive to Philadelphia.

Leaving Sandra at Melvin's, I drove to Philly. As the car ate up the road, I felt convicted determination for what I was about to do. The closer I got to my destination, the more apprehension invaded my conviction. I hadn't talked or written to Eloise since the break up. I didn't know what my reception would be when she saw me. But one thing I did know—I wasn't letting go of us without a fight.

Sitting in my car in front of Eloise's house, I paused a moment to gather my nerves. The click of my heels on the cold walkway, leading to the front door, sounded extra loud. I held my breath, waiting as the last strains of the doorbell faded.

The door locks clicked and the door swung open. My eyes rested on Eloise's mother. Her face registered surprise and shock mixed with warm kindness.

"Clifford! What a surprise. How nice to see you." She beckoned me into the house by moving her body from the doorway and standing aside. I stepped in and awkwardly extended myself for a hug. Eloise's mother had always treated me nicely. I'd always felt she approved of our relationship, and she didn't make me feel any different now.

"How have you been? Do you like Denver?" she inquired as we sat down. We chit chatted about the last few years, using small talk to skate over the obvious reason I was there. Finally, I went for the gusto.

"Is Eloise here?"

"Yes she is Clifford, up in her room." A short silence settled between Eloise's mother and me. She had mercy on me. "Why don't you go on up and see her."

Gingerly I climbed the stairs, my heart pounding in my ears louder and louder. I knocked on the bedroom door. It opened, and the face I gazed into was not the same person I'd left four years earlier.

Gone was the short, skinny Eloise with the girlish, straight up and down figure— curves and bumps still budding. Gone was the adolescent face of fleshy innocence with the rosy cuteness. Eloise stood before me, petite, but with curves and bumps in all the right places. Fully grown. Her face had mature features. She was absolutely beautiful. My chest ached.

"Clifford." Eloise stared at me with wide-eyed disbelief. "What are you doing here?"

"Hi Eloise," I stammered out. "You, really look great." I couldn't take my eyes off her. Other words I wanted to say stuck in my throat, unable to make their way past the boulder blocking their exit. Eloise and I stood as if suspended by time, our gaze glued together by the shock we both felt.

"Clifford," she said again. "What are you doing here? I mean, this is totally unexpected."

"I know Eloise, but I, I had to come see you. We need to talk."

"Talk? Talk about what?"

"Talk about us, Eloise. You and me. I want us to get back together. I've never cared about anybody else, not all the while I've been in Denver. I promised you I'd be faithful and I have

67

been. You've gotta believe me Eloise."

Exasperated, Eloise turned away, walking deeper into her bedroom. I followed her ready to continue pleading my case.

"We can't get back together Clifford. It won't work."

"Why not?"

"Because you live in Denver and I live here. It's too hard to carry a long-distance relationship. We never even see each other. I mean, we haven't seen each other in four years, and writing letters doesn't do the job."

"So, let's get married." It popped out before I barely knew what I was saying, but I meant it. Eloise was the only girl for me and I was ready to do anything to keep her in my life.

"WHAT?" Eloise whirled around, struggling to catch her breath.

"Let's get married. You can move to Denver and we won't have to worry about being separated anymore."

"NO. No, Clifford." Eloise emphatically shook her head, the impact of my suggestion still trying to sink in. I couldn't understand her hesitancy. It was a perfectly logical solution to me.

"But why not? I love you Eloise and I know you've loved me. I can take care of us. I'm working and—"

Eloise stopped me mid-sentence. She couldn't do it. We were too young, she wasn't leaving Philadelphia and going somewhere she didn't know anybody, she wasn't leaving her mother, and on and on. As she kept putting up roadblocks, I kept tearing them down. It didn't do any good.

"The answer is no, Clifford. I'm not marrying you, and that's it. I'm sorry."

I realized Eloise really was through with me. I was yesterday's news. Seeing me in person didn't change that. It was over. I had refused to accept the inevitable—like I had done with Chuck's death. But her rejection was final.

I sat in my car in front of Eloise's house, my self-esteem lying in shreds around my soul. I didn't want to go back to Ohio. I didn't want to go back home to Denver. I didn't know where I wanted to go. I just know I wanted the pain to stop. I wanted those old feelings of never being good enough, to go away. I needed to do anything to dull my senses so I wouldn't hurt so much. I needed to go somewhere. See someone.

I thought about *Audrey, one of my uncles' step-daughter. We were the same age and we'd known each other since childhood. I knew she lived in Philadelphia, so I called and told her I was in town. She invited me over.

"Hey Clifford," Audrey said, pulling me in the door with a hug. "What are you doin' in Philly?"

"I just came to see a friend and thought I'd stop by to see you and say hello."

We talked for a little while. I don't know how it happened, everything was a blur. But suddenly I found myself in Black Satin with Audrey in the passenger's seat, headed to New York. There I was, a 20-year-old country, naive kid hanging out in New York city, about to receive the biggest education of my life.

We drove to a bar run by one of Audrey's girlfriends who was a friend of the family. Walking inside was like stepping onto another planet. It was dark and I couldn't see anything at first. As my eyes adjusted to the darkness, I made out the forms of people around the room. Thick smoke burned my eyes and made it difficult to breathe.

As I looked around the room, the men and women seemed oblivious to the presence of anyone else. The couple on the floor dancing, bodies grinding against each other. The couple in a corner booth, faces close, talking, kissing, drinking, hands

*Name has been changed.

groping each other. A woman straddling a guy sitting on a chair, moving with the music. Booze flowing everywhere, and though I didn't know it, a few drugs too.

This world scared me. I didn't belong here. But it was dark enough to get lost in, and that's what I needed—to lose myself. Not completely. Just enough to forget Eloise.

I stayed in New York about a week, until I'd spent all of my money. I didn't even have a dime to buy gas. The bar owner loaned me gas money to get back to Ohio. At Melvin's house, I found Sandra already gone back to Denver. I, on the other hand, decided to stay in Oberlin to live with Melvin and his wife.

— — — — • — — — —

Living in Oberlin gave me the liberation I'd craved at home. I could finally be a man, making my own decisions and doing whatever the heck I wanted to do without explaining anything to mama and daddy. No rules, no questions.

Melvin had long since given up the Adventist lifestyle he'd learned and practiced as a child. He drank liquor and hung out, and now he had me for company. Melvin was a regular at Frank's Bar, a place where the fellas got together to drink and shoot dice.

Like a stone fool I tried my hand at shooting dice. Obviously I hadn't learned my lesson, or the skill, since my encounter with the boys from my daddy's construction crew. I lost all my money. But did that stop me? Heck, no! A week later I tried it again, always winning a few times to wet my appetite, but inevitably leaving the game broke.

Now, I look back and realize how utterly dense I was. It's plain as day now, with a free and clear mind. But at that time, all I cared about was feeling wanted. I needed somebody to make me feel accepted. And that's what the comradery of the guys at Frank's Bar did for me. Eloise didn't want me, but these guys liked me enough to include me in the group. So I did what the group did to prove I could hang.

After a few weeks of hanging out at Frank's, someone introduced me to vodka and orange juice. Until then, I had limited my drinking to Thunderbird and other "mild" alcohol, like beer. I never really liked the taste of alcohol so I never tasted the hard stuff. But vodka was different. A colorless liquid, it had no taste when mixed with orange juice. My breath didn't stink after drinking it, either.

One night I ordered a double shot of vodka and orange juice. I downed it, and ordered another double. That warm alcohol glow began filling my body and I started floating. It's called getting a buzz.

"Cliff, you'd better not drink too much of these things," Melvin warned me.

"I'm cool; I can handle it," I assured him. I drank another double.

"I'm telling you Cliff, that stuffs got a kick."

"Back off Melvin. I said I can handle it."

Who did he think he was, telling me to quit? I was feeling great! The best I had felt since my break up with Eloise. I didn't care about anything.

"Bring me another one," I heard a voice say. My brain was thinking, *bring me another one,* but I wasn't sure if I actually said it.

I downed my fourth drink. The voices in the bar sounded like people talking in a tunnel. My brain felt like mush. I couldn't get my eyes focused. I blinked hard, willing myself to see one bartender. I blinked hard again. Finally, I decided I needed some air.

I stood up to walk outside and the room moved under my

feet. I fought to keep my balance, wishing the room would stop spinning because it was making me feel sick. I kept my eyes on the door and talked one of my feet into stepping in front of the other. "One step at a time," I kept telling myself. "You can do it. You'll be fine once you get some air."

I staggered outside and almost immediately, all that vodka and juice, and anything else I may have had in my system, erupted from my mouth. My body heaved and heaved as it rejected the consumed poison. Whenever I thought I was through, my stomach wretched again and my body rattled like paper in the wind.

I'd never vomited so much in my life. There seemed to be no end. When all the alcohol was released, the vile taste in my mouth from the mixture of alcohol, sour food and stomach acid made me nauseous and I wretched again.

I don't remember Melvin taking me home. The rest of what I did remember, though, was enough that I never touched alcohol again.

————•————

The winter of 1960 was extremely cold and Melvin and I couldn't find enough work to keep busy. As a result, money was very tight. Black Satin showed her age, breaking down all the time and draining me of any money I had left. I finally sold her, ending a significant era.

Melvin co-signed for me to buy another car—a 1956, green Chevrolet Bel Air with a continental kit on the back. Yes, I was stupid, going into debt for a car I knew I couldn't make payments on. I hadn't saved any money and neither had Melvin, and work was scarce. So of course, I wasn't able to make the monthly payments. Each time I found work to make a few dollars, the jobs only lasted a few weeks.

As the months went by, the pain from my break up with

Eloise hurt less and less. I'd tried so many things to make the pain go away, when all it needed was time. And *Jackie helped too.

Jackie was the sister-in-law of one of my brothers. We'd met when I was 14 and she, a couple of years younger. Pre-Eloise, I had a crush on Jackie. Jackie, like all of her sisters, was extremely fair-skinned—so light, with such straight hair, she looked almost White. Small and petite, with an easy-going, sweet-natured personality, I considered Jackie a pretty little girl.

I hadn't seen Jackie since we were teenagers. When I discovered she lived in Cleveland, we got reacquainted. We started spending a lot of time together and eventually, I began dating her seriously.

Soon, my teenaged feelings for Jackie rekindled. The more time we spent in each other's company, the more my feelings for her deepened. Before I knew it, I loved her. And I managed to convince myself that I was also *IN* love with her.

One night we were together, I ventured again into familiar territory.

"Do you love me?" I asked Jackie.

"Of course I do, you know I do Cliff." she answered playfully.

"Then let's get married."

She laughed a nervous giggle, playfully hitting at me.

"Caliiiiff; we can't get married."

"Why not?" I grabbed her hands and held them.

"Well (pause)...well, because I'm not ready for marriage just yet."

I left it alone for right then, but not for good. Periodically I asked her to marry me, and each time she said "let's wait and see," putting me off.

I didn't know what she was waiting for. Jackie had a good

job at the telephone company, and she was great at saving her money. She kept saying she wanted a nicely furnished apartment and money in the bank before talking marriage. I began to think security was more important to her than my love.

Looking back, I know Jackie was doing the right thing. She was concerned with planning for the future and I was concerned with living for the moment. But at the time, my self-esteem was in crisis again. I never found enough work to stay steadily employed. Money was always tight, and now, again, the girl I loved didn't want to marry me.

Finally I got fed up being rejected by Jackie. How much hurt did a guy have to take? I stopped seeing her. Thoroughly unhappy and disgusted, I decided it was time to leave Ohio. There was no other place to go, but back home to Denver.

I didn't tell Melvin or anyone else that I was leaving. I just packed my clothes and pointed the green Chevy for home, unsure of where my life was headed. With no idea of what to do once I got wherever I was going.

*A prudent man sees danger
and takes refuge,
but the simple keep going and
suffer for it.*
Proverbs 22:3

Chapter 6

FAMILY MAN

I now pronounce you man and wife."

I leaned over to kiss my bride, Evelyn, as our families looked on. Hope filled me with the prospect of new beginnings—a new life. A life as a husband, with someone to love me and care for me, and a chance to return the same.

I'd known Evelyn since we were teenagers. We'd met at church, in Denver, and developed an easy acquaintance. We never hung out—I was too busy hanging with Lennie and Rick, and Eloise was still my girl. But Evelyn's and my path crossed every now and then.

Evelyn was short, light-skinned, with a medium build and big brown eyes. She was very quiet, with a calm, easy-going personality that gave her an aura of softness, and a million dollar smile. That softness, coupled with her natural friendliness, attracted me. Not to mention the fact that she was always dressed neatly. But she wasn't particularly attracted to me. I was too boisterous, too pushy. So we were just acquaintances. Fellow teens at the church. That was our only contact, until I returned home to Denver from Oberlin.

Evelyn first popped into my mind while I was driving back to Denver from Oberlin. Emotionally, I felt like crap. Jackie and I hadn't worked out, and I couldn't find work. My life had stalled. I needed to see a friendly face. I needed something to make me feel worthwhile, and that "something" always seemed to be a woman.

Last I knew, Evelyn had gone to live with her parents in Omaha, Nebraska. Since I had to go through Nebraska, I decided to stop by and pay a little visit. The closer I got, the more anticipation rose up within me. I pictured the surprised look on Evelyn's face when she saw me standing at the door. I fantasized the whole encounter, feeding the slight eagerness massaging my ego.

When I arrived, I got the surprise. Evelyn no longer lived in Omaha. She was back in Denver, living with her sister. Though disappointed for the moment, this turn of events proved even better. I vowed to look Evelyn up once I got home.

Nothing and no one in Denver had changed. I picked up right where I left off—living with my parents and their rules. Living my preferred lifestyle in secret, doing whatever I could get away with. Working, and hanging out with Lennie and Rick.

It was easy falling back in with Lennie, Rick and the rest of their crowd. I found them doing the same 'ole same 'ole, drinking, partying, and shootin' the breeze. But I added a new friend to my circle. Evelyn. I couldn't get into Denver quick enough before looking up Evelyn. The minute I discovered where she lived, I landed on her doorstep.

"Hi Clifford." Evelyn stood in the doorway, a warm smile lighting up her face. "Come on in." I stepped into her sister's house and sat down.

"It's good to see you Evelyn, it's been a while. How you doin'? You look good."

We chit-chatted—about leaving Denver, me in Ohio, her in Omaha, being back in Denver—catching up. It was easy conversation. Warm. Safe.

"This is Stephen, my son." Evelyn held her butterball baby. At five months, he already had personality, with his near toothless grin that drenched everything in sight.

"Hey man," I cooed as I reached for him. He gave me a quizzical look like "who are you," then broke into a watery grin that said if mommy thinks you're okay, then you're fine with me; as long as she's in sight. Stephen and I became instant buddies. We understood each other. It must've been a man thing.

As time went by Evelyn's friendship slowly expressed itself in ways Lennie and Rick never could. Eventually, we were spending every free minute we had, together.

Evelyn and I grew into a comfortable relationship, with Stephen at our side. We fed each other's emotional needs. She made me feel manly, I made her feel secure. I poured my need for acceptance into her soul and she responded. I was deeply "in like" with her.

One night we were together, Evelyn seemed a little distracted.

"Cliff..." Evelyn paused, mildly nervous. I watched her mind search for words, steeling myself for the inevitable—rejection. My heart pounded as I waited for her to tell me why we couldn't go on seeing each other, or that she was interested in someone else, or any of the other words all my relationships seemed to end with.

"Cliff...I'm pregnant."

Those were not the words I'd prepared myself to hear. It didn't make sense. We hadn't really had sex. I mean, we'd messed around—heavy petting and kissing—all the while trying hard to resist the urge to go full force. There was only one time—once, that any semblance of sex occurred, and that wasn't even the full-fledged thing. And here Evelyn was, telling me she's pregnant.

Immediately, my mind engaged in a battle of emotional tug-of-war. I'd gotten with Evelyn because I needed somebody in my life. Now she was telling me she's pregnant and the only right thing to do was to marry her. I cared about Evelyn and Stephen, but I wasn't sure I was ready to make a marriage commitment. But then, I felt sorry for her. She already had one son with no husband. What would people think of her having two babies and no husband. I didn't want to see her go through that kind of humiliation.

Back and forth, back and forth I volleyed with myself. In the end, I figured this could be just what I needed to give my life purpose. To prove myself. To finally do the right thing. So I did the right thing.

"Marry me Evelyn."

"What? Are you serious?"

"Yes I'm serious. "

As we talked, I convinced myself I could do this. She convinced herself it was alright. I was even willing to tell myself that I loved her, as much as I understood about love. Neither of us considered becoming a family as being all that difficult. We were practically a family already. Living together under one roof would be the single major difference.

We made plans, envisioning our life together. I wanted the same kind of "good home" I grew up in; a Christian home, raising our children with the same Adventist values I was raised with—morning and evening worship, church every week. The more we talked, the more I knew this was exactly what I needed to get back to my roots.

My confidence grew as I thought about my own family life. My father was a wonderful role model. Watching him, taught me the two most important principles that make a good husband. First, a good husband always takes care of his family. And second, family always comes first. What was I scared of? I could do that. Once Evelyn and I figured it all out, we separately told our families.

"Evelyn and I are getting married," I informed my parents one day, with a tone of finality. They didn't appear shocked. Getting married at a young age wasn't all that uncommon. But neither were they jumping up and down at the news, especially daddy.

"Clifford, do you think that's a good idea?" he asked. "She has a child that is not yours, and you'd be responsible for raising him..."

Evelyn having a child always bothered daddy when we were dating. It made no difference to me that he wasn't my blood son. I cared about Stephen as deeply as I cared about Evelyn.

Daddy continued his protest. "You don't even know her that well. Ya'll been goin' out, what, a couple of months?"

"What difference does that make?" I asked. "I love her and she loves me, and we want to be together."

Of course, my parents weren't getting the whole story. I never mentioned anything about Evelyn being pregnant with MY child. My ego wasn't ready to handle the full brunt of their shame and disappointment if they knew I'd had sex before marriage. I was protecting Evelyn's honor as well.

My folks weren't happy with my announcement. It's a parent thing. When you have kids, you fantasize what their lives will be like; who they'll marry and how it will happen. You plan it all out. But low and behold, they choose their own path. And you have to stand by and watch your children do things their way, regardless of the outcome. Many times it's a painful experience.

Mama finally stifled her and daddy's resistance. "If you marry Evelyn," she said, "I'll accept her as my daughter-in-law."

So there I stood, with my wife by my side. Transformed into a family man.

Our families had gathered at Evelyn's sister's house for our small wedding. Nothing fancy. Just a plain, simple wedding. We couldn't afford anything more. Everyone congratulated us, silently hoping that our union would "make it." I had not shown myself to be a model of stability, and we were both young. I was 21 and Evelyn was 19. It was November, 1961.

Lennie, Rick and the rest of my friends did not come to the wedding. But toward the end of the celebratory reception, I heard their cars drive up to the house.

"Ya did it huh dude. Ya done gone off and got yourself hitched," they teased good naturedly.

"Well, come on," Lennie urged, " let's celebrate. Let's show the new couple off. Let's tell everybody in Denver 'bout ya'll gettin' married."

I ran to get Evelyn so we could ride around town with the guys, sharing our good news with anyone who'd listen. Evelyn wasn't bowled over by the idea, but she agreed to go. We kissed and hugged our family members good-bye and roared off in my green Chevy Bel Air with a "Just Married" sign hung on the back. A trail of cans tied to the bumper, dragged and rattled on the ground, and my friends followed behind us in their cars.

Yelling, screaming and honking our horns, we drove through the city acting like fools. The fellas and I were having a wild and crazy good time. Evelyn quietly sat through the ride. After a while, she signaled she'd had enough.

"Cliff, I'm ready to go home."

I wasn't ready to stop the fun, especially being with my boys. I figured this to be the last time we'd really hang out, now that I was a married man. I didn't want it to end, yet. But

I had to admit, I was tired too. I waved one of the cars up to the side of mine.

"Yo fellas, we gotta go," I said a little reluctantly.

"Aw come on man, just a little while longer."

"Naw, naw. It's been a long day, man, and we're tired. So we just gonna go on home." The boys and I said our goodbyes and I headed the Chevy to my tiny apartment. My mind raced to the sound of Evelyn's breathing as she slept. It was mind boggling. I was married. I was a husband. A father and a father-to-be. In one fell swoop. I closed my eyes for sleep, still marveling at this turn of events.

In the early, early daylight I crept out of the apartment, leaving Evelyn asleep. I went out to fill an incredible urge I just couldn't shake. Surprise wrote all over mama's face when I walked through the door of my parents' house.

"What are you doing here?"

"I just wanted to come over and eat breakfast."

As I listened to the words leave my mouth, the realization that I was married smacked me, and I was overwhelmed with a cold feeling of being a fraud. I didn't want to be a husband. I really wanted to be right here—in my mother's house, asking her to feed me and take care of me, like she always did. Instead, I had a wife sleeping at home.

I felt trapped. And scared. And confused.

"Sit down," mama ordered me, proceeding to cook breakfast without another word. When the last bite of food passed my lips, mama looked me in the face, her compassionate eyes drawing my full attention.

"Son." She paused, letting the understanding sink in that I would always be her son. "You're married, and you must go home to your wife."

That simple. That powerful. The undercurrent of her emotion sucked me into all the words she didn't say. Her point was clear. I had responsibilities and I had to be right. I had to do right.

I left mama, determined to be a good husband and father just like my daddy. Exactly the way mama wanted me to be. If only determination was all it took.

———•———

"Dag-gon-it Clifford! This bill hasn't been paid." Evelyn waved the overdue bill in my face, her brow furrowed in tight little lines.

"What the heck do you want me to do Evelyn? We can't pay it right now." I snatched the bill from her fingers and threw it on top of the growing overdue pile.

"What do you mean what do I want you to do? You've got to PAY it."

"How can I PAY it with no MONEY!"

No money. My pocket had an invisible drain sucking the money out the minute I put any in. Always playing catch up, I couldn't get ahead. Denver's winter didn't offer many opportunities for construction work. So the pattern stayed the same. I'd find a job making decent money, but all the money I made paid the bills that piled up when I didn't have a job. Then, I'd go another stretch with no work. The vicious cycle continued.

"Well you'd better find a way to get some," Evelyn continued, "cause we can't keep piling these bills up, putting them in a corner, acting like they're not here."

"Well, WHAT DO YOU *THINK* I'M TRYING TO DO, HUH?!"

The tiny apartment was a pressure cooker, suffocating me. True to my habit, I grabbed my jacket and stormed out, slamming the door behind me. This scene got harder and harder to stomach. Evelyn was increasingly irritable as the pregnancy took over her body and hormones. Worrying about our lack of money only made it worse. Her irritability fed my irritability causing us to constantly argue.

This is not how I'd pictured married life. I went in with such high expectations for us, for me. We'd started off great—spending time together, building our life. Stephen was growing like a vine, and he and I had bonded. Eventually I adopted him, symbolically stamping out any division in our family.

But this is where we'd come to. Me stomping out of the house, finding solace with the fellas. Spending more and more time with them, and less and less time with my wife and child. Goodness, I just needed a break. Swallowing my pride, I did what I had to do.

Once again, standing in my parents' house, I shifted uneasily from one foot to the other. I hated asking my parents for help. Asking them for help was admitting to them I couldn't cut it as a good husband, a provider. But I was drowning and I didn't know where else to turn.

"Daddy," I took a deep breath. "Uh...Evelyn and I...uh, (cleared throat), you know we uh....are having a little trouble paying bills and uh (cleared throat), I wanted to know if uh...I could borrow some money, you know, just for a couple of weeks...I promise I'll pay you back..."

Daddy came to the rescue, loaning me whatever money he could spare. If my parents hadn't helped us on many occasions, my family would've been out on the street. Unfortunately this time, their help wasn't enough to save us.

The jobs dried up, my car broke down, and the bills continued to accumulate. Finally, we lost our apartment. Evelyn and Stephen moved to Omaha to stay with her family and I moved in with mama and daddy. For those of you who know the Bible story about Job, the man who lost everything in an instant;

you could say we were in full "Job" syndrome.

Feelings of inadequacy flicked at my senses, taunting me with my childhood thoughts of being a failure, good for nothing, worthless. I'd let Evelyn and Stephen down. I'd let mama and daddy down. I'd let me down. I was embarrassed and ashamed that my family was not together. But I couldn't let that stop me. My fierce priority became getting Evelyn and Stephen back to Denver.

For three months, I hustled. Any and every job I could find, I worked ferociously, saving money for my family. By the end of three months, I'd saved enough to get another apartment. Evelyn and Stephen came back home. I achieved what I set out to do—be a man and provide for my family. We still struggled, but we were a family again, and that's all that mattered. I determined to keep it that way. No matter what.

As the weather warmed, work became more plentiful. Just like Job in the Bible, I didn't stay down for long. I took care of the bills, and even began saving a little bit. My son, Jeffrey was born, July, 1962. I strutted like a proud peacock showing off his feathers. I loved my sons with all my heart and I worked hard to make sure they, and Evelyn had what they needed. To me, that meant material things.

Ingrained with Daddy's belief that paying rent was nothing more than living in a house with a monthly receipt, my next goal, as a good husband/father, became buying a house. As the jobs kept coming, I kept working and saving money, and we started house hunting.

After several months of looking, Evelyn and I found the perfect house. It was a beautiful, three-bedroom brick home on a corner lot. If there was any negative aspect about the house, it could've been the fact that we would be the only Black family in the entire neighborhood. But that was more of a downside for the neighbors, not for us.

After securing the $800 down payment, which I borrowed from my employer, I moved my family into "Harris Mansion." We didn't care that the neighborhood residents didn't treat us very friendly. We were proud owners of our very own home.

I was equally proud of myself and what I'd accomplished. I knew if I could just get the breaks, I could be the man my daddy taught me to be—the provider, the caretaker, hardworking. Buying this house proved it. But I even took it one step further. I involved myself with my children.

I took pleasure spending time with Stephen, Jeffrey, and later, my daughter Rhonda. I loved watching them grow—sitting up by themselves for the first time, discovering their fingers and toes, taking their first steps, exploring the simple, innocent facets of life with intense curiosity. We played games and went places together. I felt important, knowing that I was giving my children something my daddy rarely gave me—time. Life was good. I was living the family picture I had mentally started my marriage with. Except for the spiritual aspect.

Starting out, I planned to have a Christian home. I dreamed of having morning and evening worship—just like my daddy had done with my family. I planned to attend church every week, just like I had grown up doing. But I found it a little hard playing the role of "priest" in my house. I didn't like having to lead out. Reading daily devotionals was hard because I couldn't read well. It reminded me how educationally inadequate I was, and I didn't want my children seeing that.

Every once in a while we'd go to church as a family, but Evelyn didn't really care for the people. She always felt sensitive about her spotted past, knowing that some members had used her history as common discussion material. We never stayed after the service to chit-chat with anyone. Before the preacher could barely end his sermon, we were out the door going back home. With no real support from Evelyn, my dreams of family spirituality quickly fell to the side of the road. Sometimes I felt guilty, but most times I tried not to think about it. We were doing okay financially and physically. But without a spiritual connection, our family unit was about to slowly come apart.

— — — —•— — — —

"I'm going out," I told Evelyn one evening, heading for the door.

"So what's new," she responded without looking at me.

"Man Evelyn, why you got to be like that?" I knew she resented my hanging out, but I felt I deserved some fun every now and then after working so hard all the time.

"Because you could spend a little more time with your family. Seems like you're always gone."

What Evelyn wanted to say is that I should spend more time with her, which was probably true. But we were total opposites. I enjoyed being around people—laughing, joking, going out and just having a good time. Evelyn was shy and reserved. I needed more than just working and coming home, being husband and daddy. Evelyn was a homebody. So, since Evelyn and I had no real friends as a couple, I hung out with the fellas. Which was the other part of the problem.

Evelyn hated my circle of friends. She felt they were bad influences, just bringing me down. She didn't know Lennie, Rick and my other friends actually kept me going. Unfortunately for me though, in order to keep hanging around them, I needed to feel accepted by them. That meant, I had to do what they were doing, which was the beginning of the end.

"Here," Lennie said one day, casually handing me a joint. "You want to mellow out, man and just forget any s— you go

86

through? Just try this."

I took the joint between my fingers, a super-thin, rolled up cigarette with a sweet, pungent odor coming from the smoke wafting from its tip. I'd never smoked marijuana before. I hadn't smoked anything before, though all the guys smoked cigarettes and marijuana—weed—all the time.

I didn't know much about weed, except that if the cops caught us with a single seed they'd slam our butts in jail. Possessing marijuana was a felony in those days. Society totally disapproved of weed. Regardless, I wanted the same mellowness my friends always got after a few hits. I wanted to look like them, be one of the guys.

"Yeah, sure," I said, trying to sound confident. "I'll give it a try."

I put the tip of the paper between my lips, inhaling deeply, like you do when the doctor wants to listen to your chest with his stethoscope. Mimicking my friends, I held my breath a few seconds, letting the smoke's potency burn deep into my lungs. Then I slowly exhaled.

Lennie and I sat there, passing the joint back and forth between us. I didn't feel any different after my first drag. But after a few more, I became a new man. All of a sudden, the clouds rolled back and the sun shone bright. A beautiful warm wind whooshed me off the ground, lifting me up, up.

The higher I went, the smaller my troubles became. Soon, they looked like ants. The same way houses and cars look when airplanes get farther and farther from land. I waved good-bye. I was flying high.

My body relaxed. I started to laugh; I don't know why. No one made a joke. No one said anything funny. I just, laughed. For no particular reason. Everything was funny. You could have said, "Cliff your pants are on fire!", and I would've laughed. Nothing was important. Best of all, I felt great.

"Man, this s— is good," I said, reaching for the joint and inhaling again. "This is the life." I had no idea how prophetic those words were.

Initially, I only smoked weed occasionally with my friends. I refused to smoke it in my car or in my house. I didn't want Evelyn or the children involved in my social activities. Evelyn would just give me grief, and the children didn't need to know how I lived my life outside of the house.

Eventually, I went from an occasional smoke, to smoking with my friends all the time, to buying my own stash. Weed slowly became part of my groove. It was socially bonding, something willingly shared between friends. There was nothing more intimate than sitting with my fellas, passing a joint from hand to hand, communing with each other about life.

I did not perceive my growing dependency on weed. I wasn't physically dependent, because the body does not suffer without it—but mentally and emotionally dependent. Weed took the edge off my stress when the mood in my house wasn't so good. It kept me mellow, allowing me to perform my family duties with calm and clarity. But hard as I tried, I couldn't keep my home life and street life from crossing each other.

One sun-shiny, beautiful warm Denver day, I was washing my car in the driveway. Three-year-old Jeffrey kept me company outside, doing what comes naturally to toddlers—exploring.

We played our share of games, Jeffrey climbing through the car, me chasing him with the water hose, hide and seek. He mimicked me every now and then, using his little rag to scrub the same spot on the car. Soon he got bored and sauntered around looking for some new adventure to occupy his fertile mind.

"What you doin' Jeffrey?" I asked periodically, when the air got too quiet or if he was out of eyesight. "Nuffin," his pip-squeak voice chirped back, his eyes peeking around the edge of the car door, or the corner of the rear bumper. "Alright, make sure you stay where daddy can see you," I admonished.

Engrossed in my chore, it was a while before I realized the air was too still. "Jeffrey," I called, "what you doin'?" No answer. "Where are you Jeffrey?"

"I right here, daddy."

I looked over the car to see my son merrily emptying out a plastic bag onto the grass. With each jerk and swing of his hand, the bag's contents spilled across the ground, specks of residue softly gliding through the air.

"JEFFREY," I yelled, when the surrealism vanished and the reality of what was happening broadsided me. Jeffrey had found my bag of reefer stashed in the car, and was pouring it out on the grass.

Blindly abandoning whatever I held in my hand, I charged toward my son. I grabbed his arm as the last of the reefer floated away. Immediately, I was furious and pitiful in the same instant. Thoughts raced through my head like rapid fire. *Why couldn't Jeffrey have emptied the bag on the cement, at least I would have been able to save it; there was my good high gone in a poof, camouflaged in the grass; how dare Jeffrey waste my money; I need to teach him a lesson; he can't just go messing with things that aren't his.*

Angrily I yanked Jeffrey to me, yelling in his face. "DIDN'T DADDY TELL YOU TO STAY WHERE I COULD SEE YOU? HUH? DIDN'T I?!" Swiftly, I reached down and began spanking him, words tumbling from my mouth with each pop. Words that were all lies.

My son thought he was getting spanked for disobedience, or for taking something that wasn't his, or for any justifiable excuse I could come up with depicting his flagrant disregard for my commands. When really, each lash of my hand—crusted by years of manual labor—connecting with his supple, baby skin, was really for the delicious high I eagerly anticipated getting later that evening, suddenly blown to pieces by his innocent act of curiosity.

I ordered Jeffrey into the house, wanting to be alone to feel sorry for myself and my lost high. Never realizing, until now—looking back and replaying that scene with a clear, sober mind—how my choices were already infiltrating family territory, quietly setting the stage for the family's eventual demise.

He who trusts in himself is a fool, but he who walks in wisdom is kept safe.
Proverbs 28:26

Chapter 7

FOOT IN HELL

A s long as I kept a job, the family existed in relative peace. The money I made paid the current bills. Nothing more. Nothing less. There was no extra, no cushion. Each month we eked by was a triumphant relief. But never getting ahead began to fester in me like an open sore.

Tired of barely making it, Evelyn started a discussion we'd had several times already.

"Clifford. I want to get a job."

I sucked my teeth. "Dang Evelyn. We've been all through that. You don't need no job."

No matter how many times we talked about this, my answer remained the same. This time, though, Evelyn wouldn't let the issue go.

"Clifford, we need more money coming into the house, and I want to work. IBM is opening up a new plant in Boulder and I've got a real good chance of getting on with them." She tried to temper her excitement, knowing I wasn't going to go for it.

"I don't care Evelyn. You don't need to work. You ain't supposed to work. That's what men do, not women. It ain't right."

"Oh puhlease Cliff," Evelyn sucked her teeth, rolling her eyes. "That's ridiculous. Lots of women work."

"Well you ain't lots of women. You're MY wife and you ain't working. I'm the man of the house and it's MY responsibility to provide for my family."

"This isn't about you and what you're supposed to do,"

Evelyn contended. "This is about me and my being tired of just sitting around the house doing nothing. This job would help us get ahead financially, provide insurance for the kids, and—"

"We're doing fine, Evelyn. I don't need you going out and working. That's my job and I'm doing it. Your job is to take care of us. Period."

I still held on to my adolescent definition of what makes a man, though I was 27 years old. And what would you expect in 1967? All men defined "manhood" the same way. Women stayed home and cared for the family. Men went out and worked to provide for the family.

"Well I'm sorry, Cliff. Staying home is a job that's not enough for me." Evelyn turned away signaling the end of the conversation. Ignoring my wishes, Evelyn applied for a job at IBM anyway and they hired her. I took it as the ultimate insult. She was infringing on MY duties as a husband and father.

I didn't care about Evelyn needing fulfillment in her life other than taking care of the kids and the house. That wasn't even an issue for men back then. It didn't matter that we financially eked by. The only issue for me was that I was the provider, the caretaker, and Evelyn encroached on my space.

To add insult to injury, IBM put Evelyn on the night shift which meant I had to stay home and take care of the kids. I couldn't hang out with the fellas anymore. I stayed home and gave the children dinner, and baths, and bedtime stories. Then sat around and watched T.V. after they went to bed. My ego couldn't handle the house-husband label forced on my manhood.

Evelyn's job drove the final wedge between her and me. We hardly saw each other; and when we did, we were always biting each other's head off. I resented her, and she resented me resenting her. She viewed herself as helping me out, easing the family's financial burden, easing my pressures. I viewed her as muscling in on my program, challenging my manhood, messing up my recreation. And when I did have a chance to hang out, usually on the weekends, she always said something about it.

"You always talking bad about Lennie and Rick, and I'm SICK of it," I yelled at her the next time she bucked at my going out. "They are MY friends, whether you like it or not." Evelyn's indictment against my friends was an indictment against me. I felt if she thought they were no good, then she thought I was no good, too.

The more we drove each other away, the more solace I sought in weed. The calm I felt after smoking a joint gave me the courage to go back home and face the tension. Ever so slowly, the smoking escalated. Soon I stayed high all the time—smoking two or three joints after work, smoking joints on the way to work. Eventually, Evelyn caught on that I was into something, but she didn't know what.

Once again, work hit a sporadic spell. But this time was different. Evelyn had power, because Evelyn had a job. Little by little, she took control of the family. She guarded the money she brought in, like a hawk. She paid the bills, made decisions on how to spend the money, and budgeted. The more she took over, the less she respected me, and the less I respected myself.

A glass bottle held me captive. I went round and round in circles, fighting to get out. I liked the extra money coming in from Evelyn's job. It spent just as good as my paycheck. But each time she got paid was a finger pointing in my face, accusing me of being a failure. My mother never worked. My daddy was man enough to take care of her and us kids. But I couldn't cut it.

Every now and then, my wounded pride asserted itself. I'd rant and rave about her working, saying stuff like, "YOU are the one who's supposed to stay home and take care of the kids, not me. I am the man. I'm in charge."

Evelyn just ignored my tantrums like a parent stepping over a child sprawled out on the floor.

"Forget it Cliff," she'd say, "I'm not giving up my job. I enjoy working, and I enjoy knowing we've got a little cushion."

Evelyn's disregard for me made me feel disrespected. I didn't feel needed. I didn't feel important. I didn't feel in control. As a result, I didn't care what Evelyn felt about anything. I did what I wanted, went where I wanted with whom I wanted, and bought what I wanted—like the black on black, four-door Cadillac I got in Cincinnati, Ohio during one of my out-of-town job excursions. Evelyn despised that car, but so what. I wanted it, so I got it.

I never talked to anyone about the marital problems I struggled with, not even Lennie and Rick. But they knew something was going on, and I depended on them to make me feel good, no matter what. They understood me. They knew where I was comin' from. They gave me respect. They introduced me to weed which, up 'til now, made me feel good. But even those good feelings didn't last, as the tension at home threatened to snap me in half like a rotten twig. Accusing thoughts of being a failure ate me alive. I couldn't stand the voices inside my head that wouldn't shut up.

Instead of paying attention to the soft small voice in my chaotic head telling me all I needed was to get my spiritual act together, I ignored it, turning once again to the outside. Turning to my "true friends," Lennie and Rick.

When the impact of weed's high gradually lessened, Lennie

introduced me to a new high—pills—or "fender benders" as we called them. All kinds of pills; Red devils, Yellow jackets, Christmas trees, that we popped like M&Ms. While under the influence of these fender benders, I tore up that pretty Cadillac I cherished—driving at 2:00 in the morning, just banging into parked cars.

Once inside the grip of a high, I just wanted to keep feeling that way. I wanted to feel even better. I reached out to anything different, anything new. And I found that better high—but I stepped into hell to get it.

————•————

"Hey Cliff, lemme show you something we got going on here, man," Lennie said one night when we were together. It was 1968.

I moved closer to Lennie to see what he was doing. Crouched over a short, stubby candle with a flat bottom, he was in deep concentration. One flick of a match and the flame licked the air, setting it aglow.

With one hand, Lennie grabbed a blackened, mutilated spoon by its jagged handle edge once hidden by a long, slender handle with a rounded or artistically crafted tip. The spoon head was drastically curved so when you held it by its deformity, it was like holding a teacup.

In his other hand, Lennie held the tiniest cellophane bag I'd ever seen. Cocking it to one side, he tapped the bag with one finger, conscientiously coaxing a brownish powder into the mutilated spoon so as not to cause one grain to miss its mark.

As I watched, transfixed by the scene playing out before me, my mind propelled my memory back to snatches of overheard conversations of my friends talking about heroin—H, scag, boy, horse, or dope.

With the flick of a match, Lennie transformed our surroundings into a "shooting gallery," the place where heroin users prepare the drug and shoot it into their bodies. Littered around him were his "works"—a syringe full of water with a stainless steel needle attached to the end; anything that could wrap around your arm—usually a woman's stocking; the matches and the spoon.

While voices echoed in my mind, Lennie continued his mission. Quickly. Quietly. He meticulously squirted the water from the syringe, a thin stream of purity adulterated in the bed of the spoon by the powder waiting to defile it. Lennie held the spoon over the match, waving the flame back and forth being careful not to let the mixture boil, just heat. A stank odor permeated from the spoon.

Anticipation oozed from Lennie's pores, electrifying the molecules surrounding us. I observed his ritual, suspended in the same trance I'd experienced as a child the first time I saw guys shooting dice. Everything I'd heard my friends talk about, Lennie acted out in front of my eyes. I graduated from disinterested eavesdropper to active spectator.

Once satisfied by his creation, and after a good vomit, Lennie deftly rolled a tiny piece of cotton between his fingers. Dropping it onto the spoon, the cotton absorbed the heated liquid and residue. Taking the needle, Lennie stuck the point into the wet cotton, drawing the mixture into the syringe. He tied the stocking around his forearm, using his teeth in concert with his hand to tighten the vice's grip.

"Yeah man," Lennie's voice pierced the silence, startling me. "This makes you forget all the s—— in your life, man." I stared at the needle he picked up, its sharp point glistening in the light. Lennie closed his fist real tight, his bicep muscle bulging from his arm, the vein straining underneath his skin.

"You ain't had no high 'til you done this," he said. I watched the brown liquid slosh against the sides of the syringe. The needle point punctured his soft skin as he slid it into his arm, a little blood bubble bursting from the tiny wound. "This is the ULTIMATE high," he said, forcing the liquid from the plastic tube into his bloodstream.

In my mind's eye I could feel his blood coursing through his body with every heartbeat, carrying the drug with it. My own body tingled as I imagined the sensation he must be feeling now.

"HEY CLIFF." Lennie's words jolted me out of my dream. "You want to try it?"

I looked at the needle, hesitating. This heroin stuff seemed to be the move. Everybody loved it. They swore by it. Guaranteed to be the best high ever, "the ultimate" as Lennie said.

"CLIFF?"

"Yeah...yeah, I'll try it." I silenced that small voice sounding off in my head again, determined to try this stuff.

Lennie repeated the ritual. After the dope cooked, he showed me how to "tie up" my arm tight enough to make the vein pop up. Satisfied with the preparation, Lennie handed me the needle.

I held it in my hand and I froze. No matter how much my mind willed me, I couldn't plunge the needlepoint into my own arm. I don't know why. Maybe I couldn't stomach the thought of inflicting physical pain on myself, even though I knew the needle's sting would last only an instant. Maybe I hadn't silenced that small voice after all, and we were arguing in my head. Maybe God was holding my hand back with an invisible grip, giving me one last chance to listen and save myself from the path I was about to step on.

Whatever it was, I couldn't do it. I couldn't stick the needle in my arm.

"Here, I can't," I said to Lennie, handing him the syringe. "You do it for me."

I watched the cold, steel point break through my flesh. Blood seeped from the small wound, crawling into the syringe as Lennie pulled the plunger back. As he pushed the plunger forward, the blood flowed back into my arm, taking the heroin with it.

Instantly my body exhaled all its tension and stress with a deep "ahhhh." I was a human rag doll. Relaxation poured over me, producing a stupor that eventually made me nod off in blissful sleep. My heart raced and I could feel each pump, pump, pump as the beats forced the drug through my blood stream.

I had never, in all my life, felt this good, this peaceful, this euphoric. I had no worries. No problems. No hurt. No guilt. I had escaped. For the next few hours I was free.

But the minute the high wore off, reality's full ugliness crashed back into focus. I hadn't changed anything, or accomplished anything. The bills were still there. The arguments with Evelyn were still there. My failures were still there. This only made me want to escape again and again, into the euphoric vacuum of that powerful first heroin high. And therein is the magic of heroin. Its magic is in the lies—inconspicuously created, so willingly believed.

There is no escape from reality, just a shifting away of the eyes choosing to focus elsewhere. There is no getting back that first heroin high, just a chasing of the ghost. And by the time you realize that what you wanted to believe as truth is really a lie, your body is hooked, and terribly unforgiving when the drug is out of its system too long. It's a vicious circle, an icy grip, a desperate delusion. And it changes everything.

Instantly.

For a long time, I only used heroin if Lennie was around to do the injection. If he wasn't around, I used weed or pills to get my high on, to escape real life. I constantly chased the ghost at full speed.

Within a few weeks I knew all the regular drug dealers. I bought pills everyday. Whatever money I had during working times, I invested in making myself feel good. I had to, because no one else was going to pay for my high. When it comes to heroin, friends get stingy. Nobody shares their heroin stash. It's too precious.

So I became my sole responsibility. To me, Evelyn didn't exist. I ignored her. I stopped giving her money to help support the family. Since she wanted control, I gave it to her, confident that she would succeed where I had failed so miserably.

The children didn't exist, either. I ignored them. No more games, no more going out, no more involvement. My family died. I ignored them all, absenting myself from family activities, spinning myself into a cocoon. The house became my rest stop—a place to sleep a few hours, eat a meal, and leave.

Piece by piece, I surrendered myself to dope, until my entire being lay at its mercy. I became a puppet whose every movement, gesture, thought and word operated under dope's control. It pulled my strings. All moral, ethical, and sensible control I'd ever possessed, were wrested away by the irresistible urges that shocked every fiber of my body when I went too long without a heroin fix.

When work dried up, I didn't worry about finding another job. That took too much time and effort—time and effort that could be spent getting money an easier way, like beggin' for it.

"Evelyn, I need some money," I said one day on my way out the door.

"I don't have any money, Cliff."

"Whachu mean, you don't have no money? You got a job don'tcha? Ain't that why you wanted to work, so you could have some money?"

Evelyn's instincts told her I was up to no good. I was not the same man she'd married, at least from what she could see on the outside. She didn't know what was happening to me, but she knew it wasn't positive and she didn't trust me.

"Where's your money Cliff? Aren't you workin'? Why don't you have any money? Huh? What you doin' with it Cliff? You ain't payin' no bills, 'cause I pay the bills, Cliff. You ain't bringing no food or clothes in the house for the kids or me. Heck, you ain't even in this house more than to use it as some kind of truck stop or motel. You just sleep, eat, change your clothes and go off again, doing God only knows what!"

Evelyn's face screwed up in disgust, frustration oozing from her pores. The more she thought about what I was doing, the madder she got, anger's redness coloring her pale brown skin. Her eyes begged me for an explanation. Why was I never home? Why did I ignore the kids? Why did I ignore her? Why didn't I want to make love anymore? Why wasn't I around to play catch or ride bikes with the kids, or go on a picnic with the family? Why?

"Dag Evelyn, I didn't ask you all that. You know how my jobs come and go, and right now I'm in between jobs. I got some business I need to take care of so I need a few bucks, okay."

"No Cliff." Evelyn shook her head placing one hand on her hip, waving me away with the other.

"Whatchu mean, NO?"

"I mean NO Cliff. I ain't gonna just HAND you MONEY TO WASTE. I'm working TOO HARD making ends meet. I CAN'T

EVEN COVER all the bills we have Cliff. I'm not GIVIN' YOU ANYTHING when YOUR KIDS almost have nothing. YOU WANT SOME MONEY, YOU GO GET A DAGGONE JOB CLIFF, BECAUSE I'M NOT GIVING YOU ONE PENNY."

The front door crashed behind me as I slammed it shut, cursing Evelyn under my breath. All this crap was her fault, anyway. If she hadn't defied me and gotten a job forcing me to be with the kids all the time, I wouldn't feel like a failure. She should be supporting her man, treating me with respect. Instead, she's the one driving me to do drugs; refusing to give me money because I haven't been able to find work. Doesn't she know if I could, I'd be at a job right now making my own money?

This is a common train of thought for drug addicts. Everybody else is at fault. Something, or someone else pushes you to do drugs. The blame is never placed on the one with whom it belongs—self. Why? Because you're too emotionally fragile to accept it. To accept blame means to admit guilt, and admitting guilt makes you feel lousy. So, you talk yourself into believing it's someone else's fault.

So what, Evelyn had refused to give me money, but that wasn't going to stop me from getting my high. She wasn't the only way to get money. I just figured out another way to get what I needed, and it didn't take too long to decide what to do.

I began stealing.

It started in my own house. Since Evelyn refused to give me money, I decided to pawn anything of value for the few dollars I needed to buy my drugs.

"Where's the T.V.?" Evelyn asked me one day. I couldn't answer her. Didn't want to answer her. I wasn't good at lying, so I said nothing.

"CLIFF! WHERE IS THE T.V.?" Evelyn said a little more

forcefully. She wasn't going to let it go until I answered her question, so I told the truth.

"I pawned it."

"You did WHAT?"

"I PAWNED it at the pawn shop."

"WHY?

"YOU WOULDN'T GIVE ME ANY MONEY LIKE I ASKED AND I NEEDED SOME, SO I TOOK IT TO THE PAWN SHOP."

Evelyn looked like a crystal glass shattering into tiny pieces. Her eyes, filled with fury and hate, glared at me through the tears streaming down her cheeks. She looked at me like I was some crazed animal preying on its own flesh and blood.

"Give me the receipt," she said evenly, her voice like steel. Grabbing it from my hand she walked out of the house, returning with the television a little while later. Setting it down in its usual spot, she faced me defiantly.

"If you ever touch this T.V. again, your permanent home will be in the street."

I knew I had pushed Evelyn to the brink. She drew a line in the sand and dared me to cross it. I didn't want to leave home. After all, it was still my home too. This was still my family. I was still the father and husband. So I didn't touch the T.V. again. I just pawned the vacuum cleaner, typewriter, toaster, and anything else I could get money for.

Soon stealing from the house was too much of a headache. It kept Evelyn and the kids upset, and no matter how low I sank, I didn't want to make them a part of the life I was living. I still wanted to be a good father. I still wanted to do right. I continued to fantasize about the family going to church, about family outings, about a family unified with common goals. But I wouldn't be able to accomplish those dreams until I felt good about myself. And the only way I felt good about myself was when I was high.

So I started stealing from other people.

I did some of my best stealing from large construction sites. With so many workers around it was easy to put on a hard hat and mingle in, posing as one of the employees. Nobody ever asked me who I was or why I was there. They assumed I was an employee.

I stole drills, electric saws, power tools—anything easily carried away. I pawned my loot for whatever I could get. It didn't matter if the money reflected the actual value of the merchandise. All I wanted was enough cash to buy my dope.

My home away from home was Five Points, a section of Denver where a lot of drug addicts hung out on the corners. The police knew all about us. They knew I was married and owned my own home. They knew I worked sometimes, but not often. They were always watching us, waiting to see something suspicious before actually confronting us.

I kept my activities under wraps for the first couple of years. Like many other addicts, I did a lot of my heroin activity in a dope house or shooting gallery—a regular house, sometimes broken down and abandoned—where you didn't have to worry about being exposed shooting up on the streets or in public parks.

The dope house was infested with people. Walking to a room was like walking through a puzzle maze—bodies sprawled everywhere of people passed out or sleep. Those shooting up were oblivious to anyone else in the room, their full concentration on finding a vein to transport their high.

It was nothing to see somebody jabbing themselves for twenty minutes, trying to find an arm vein that hadn't collapsed. But the arm wasn't the only place to shoot. I watched people shoot drugs through the underside of their tongue, through their sex organs, or even in the side of their necks.

This is how I lived my life outside of the house. The deeper I sank, the stronger my demonic desires grew. As they wrested control away from me, I was powerless to keep myself from responding, doing whatever I needed to do to appease them.

My desires drove me to the point that I could no longer keep my personal life from colliding head on with the lives of my family.

...each one is tempted when, by his own evil desire, he is dragged away and enticed. Then, after desire has conceived, it gives birth to sin; and sin, when it is full-grown, gives birth to death.
James 1:14,15

Chapter 8

INTO THE DEPTHS

As the '70s rolled in, I was ravished by insatiable cravings for drugs. My family tried to live some normalcy of life, around me. Evelyn was the glue, keeping the house and the children running, without my help, and she was tired.

On one of the rare times we were home at the same time, Evelyn finally found the courage to confront me.

"Clifford," she paused, her anger churning just beneath her exterior.

"What?"

"Clifford, are you using drugs?"

Immediately fortress walls shot up around me, shielding me from the unspoken accusations implied in her question.

"WHAT? You gotta be kidding."

"No I'm not kidding, and answer my question. ARE YOU USING DRUGS?"

"Oh Evelyn, that is CRAZY! NO, I'm not using drugs," I said with "righteous" indignation. "I can't believe you even asked me that. Drugs are STUPID."

Evelyn looked at me, caught between her gut instinct and my forceful denial. Caught between the reality of what she saw, and the reality of the words spouting from my lips. I relentlessly concentrated my efforts to convince her I was telling the truth, regardless of the fact that I had used heroin less than an hour earlier.

"Goodness Evelyn, I can't believe you really think I would

get into something as bad as drugs."

"What else am I supposed to think Clifford? I don't even know who you are anymore."

Evelyn spilled her guts, unwilling to contain them any longer. She begged for an explanation as to why I wasn't working anymore. She demanded to know why I neglected her and the children. She pointed out my gaunt body, pasty skin and lips, my unkempt appearance. She railed against my erratic behavior. Why was I gone for days at a time, with no explanation.

Her words drudged up painful pictures that flashed through my mind. My daughter's eyes pleading for me to pay her some attention. The tortured expressions of my sons when I refused their entreaties to play, or to go, or to do with them. Guilt bubbled in my core like vomit churning in an upset stomach. I fought it back, swallowing it down with fury at Evelyn for making me feel bad again.

No matter what my lips said, there was no denying my actions. With each step into hell, I took a piece of my family with me. My children's innocence. My wife's dignity. My family's trust. Nobody was exempt. Regardless, I emphatically denied Evelyn's accusations and she finally dropped the subject.

Not working, I spent each waking moment devising schemes to get money. Sometimes, the opportunity just fell into my lap. Like the time Evelyn's sister, *Doretha, came from Omaha for a visit.

I had always liked Doretha, and was genuinely glad to see her, greeting her with an affectionate bear hug. She was going to be great company for Evelyn, making her focus her attention on something other than me and what I was or wasn't doing.

One day I came home for my usual pit stop, going into our bedroom. I noticed a purse lying on the bed, just beckoning me

*Name has been changed.

for a look. Tempting me to open it up. Rummaging through its contents, I discovered it was Doretha's purse, nicely stocked with a little cash. Without a real thought, I took every dollar and left the house. The next day when I returned home, Evelyn confronted me.

"What did you do with Doretha's money?" Evelyn used my face as a dartboard for the darts shooting from her eyes. She was already beyond furious.

"What do you mean what did I do with Doretha's money? I don't even know what you're talking about."

"Right Cliff, don't give me that crap. Doretha's purse was sitting on this bed this afternoon when you came in here. After you were gone, she discovered all her money missing. You were the only one in this room."

"Oh, so because nobody else came in here you accuse ME of taking the money?"

Something in Evelyn snapped and she began screaming and yelling.

"I'm SICK OF THIS CLIFFORD. HOW COULD YOU DO THIS? I CAN'T BELIEVE YOU WOULD SINK SO LOW. YOU ARE REALLY SICK, YOU HEAR ME? YOU ARE SICK AND YOU NEED HELP."

I vehemently denied her accusation.

"OH, SO YOU DON'T BELIEVE ME EVELYN? DAG! I SAID I DIDN'T TAKE DORETHA'S MONEY. YOU REALLY BELIEVE I WOULD STEAL FROM YOUR SISTER, MY OWN SISTER-IN-LAW? HOW DO YOU KNOW SHE DIDN'T USE HER MONEY? WHAT KIND OF MAN DO YOU THINK I AM?"

Evelyn's face contorted in rage and pain. Clearly, she didn't believe me no matter how hard I denied the truth. Even though neither she nor Doretha could prove my guilt, they knew without a doubt I'd stolen the money. So who was I lying to?

When the opportunity came for a real job, working construction, I took it. I was a little tired of hustling for money, and tired of beating myself up for neglecting my family. Besides, a real job insured a regular paycheck, which guaranteed me uninterrupted highs.

One Sunday night, my partner, Rick, and I went on one of our routine outings. Each of us armed with our own drug supply, we walked inside the dope house. The air smelled putrid from the odor of cooked heroin, but it didn't take long to adapt to it. After all, we were used to it.

"Here ya go, man," I said, handing the person running the house fifty cents to use a syringe. Sometimes the house charged a dollar for a syringe. Navigating our way through the halls, we found a room. I picked up an empty syringe lying on a coffee table. Fresh blood from the last user sat in a tiny puddle at the bottom of the tube.

I squirted the blood out and swished the syringe with a little water. Sometimes when I did this, I was struck by the depths to which I'd fallen, wondering how I—a man raised in a Christian, godly home—had sunk so low, where even filthy needles didn't stop me from shooting up.

Walking away from the house, both of us flying high as a kite, Rick started shaking his head.

"Man, we gotta stop this s—. We can't keep doing this. Look where we are, man. This is messed up. We messed up."

"Yeah, you right."

"Nah man, I'm serious."

"No, I know you serious, man. I'm serious too."

And I was serious. I saw what I was doing to my wife and three kids. I saw what I was doing to myself. I knew my life was messed up and I wanted to get out of this vice. Get things back to the way they used to be.

"Tell you what," Rick continued "let's stop this s— man. Let's do it together. You and me. We can help each other."

The longer we talked, the more pumped we got. We weren't addicts. We could lick this thing. We both wanted to change, bad. If we supported each other, we could quit. As we parted, we vowed that we were through. We would never use again, and we meant it.

All through that week, I valiantly fought my demons, fighting through my heroin cravings. On Thursday night, the next time I hooked up with Rick, we compared notes.

"How you doin' bro?" I asked him. "Using?"

"H— no man, I ain't used all week." He grinned a victor's smile. "You?"

"Not one drop in my veins, man."

Giddily, we congratulated each other on being clean, slapping five.

"We're going to beat this thing," Rick said with conviction.

"You d— right. This time I'm gonna help pay some bills at home." I thought about the light bill and the gas bill and the house note that needed to be paid. We didn't have any food in the house. But on Friday—payday— for the first time in a long time, I'd be able to buy some.

As I drove home Thursday night, good and evil engaged in a fierce battle. Just thinking about payday set me on edge. With nervous excitement I thought about the high I could get with all that money. The more I feasted on the thought, the more anxious I got.

NO, I told myself. I'm not gonna do it. If I do, I will spend all night shooting up and be dead broke by Saturday morning. I have quit. I've done good all week and I can't blow it now. But you don't have to blow it. Just get a little bit—like a $25 bag. Just enough to take the edge off.

All day Friday, demonic urges raged through me, beating me down. With pay in hand, I found myself propelled to the dope house. I'll only get a $25 bag, I determined. Then I'll give the rest of the money to Evelyn. That'll make her happy, and prove to her that I really am sorry for everything I've done.

But my conscience wasn't through with me yet. As I put one foot on a step and one hand on the railing to walk toward the door of the dope house, I stopped cold.

A small voice in my head said "CLIFFORD. You know when you go INSIDE THAT HOUSE, you are NOT going to spend just $25. It's going to be the SAME as it was LAST weekend, and the WEEKEND BEFORE THAT, and ALL THE OTHER WEEKENDS. You're going to spend ALL YOUR MONEY and it's going to be GONE by Saturday morning. Just like ALWAYS."

Paranoia infiltrated my brain, as I thought about the police who could be watching me right now. Someone pushed my brain's rewind button. I heard all the lies I told Evelyn and the children, and my parents; saw the ugly scenes of my gradual demise in all its splendor. In graphic detail.

I was at full-scale war. For about a minute, good and evil clashed for my soul, tearing me apart. "LOOK AT ALL THE ROTTEN THINGS YOU'VE DONE CLIFFORD," evil said. Guilt and shame seeped into the battle. I was too far gone to change now. I had done too much.

Another voice came back. Clear and concise. "GET OUT OF HERE CLIFFORD. GO ON HOME." I had already successfully beaten back my urges for five whole days. I could do it. Besides, I'd promised Rick. We had quit.

With every fiber of my body and soul poised to respond to my decision, I took a step—up to the next stair, and the next, and the next. I walked into the dope house and closed the door behind me.

I emerged Sunday night and headed for home. Sweaty, dirty, stinky, hungry, and broke. With no valid explanation to give my wife or my children. Evil won, and that's all I had to show for it.

— — — — • — — — —

As heroin locked its jaws around my flesh, the more desperate I became. When she called, I answered.

One night, Rick and I badly needed a heroin fix, but as usual, neither of us had any money. Driving around the streets of Denver trying to figure out how to get some cash, we saw an opportunity.

"Well, looky there," Rick said, nodding his head toward a late-model Lincoln pulling into a nearby parking lot. A middle-aged couple sat inside. As they got out of the car, we noticed they were dressed in evening wear—the man in a tuxedo and the woman in an evening gown.

"Let's hit 'em," I said to Rick. "They're out for an evening on the town. You know they got cash."

"Cool." Rick pulled our car behind theirs. Grabbing my brick hammer, I jumped out and walked right up to the man, standing to his side. Rick was close behind, holding a gun down by his side. Always the front man doing all the talking, I put on my meanest I-ain't-playin-with-you face.

"Gimme your money!"

The man just looked at me without moving.

"YOU DEAF? I SAID GIVE ME YOUR D— MONEY, MAN."

He still didn't move. An angry cloud covered his face as he stood defiantly, not moving a muscle. His lack of fear drove me crazy.

"YOU SON OF ..." I continued screaming at him, using

every nasty, filthy curse word known to man. After my tirade, the man still didn't move. I raised my brick hammer threateningly in his face like I was getting ready to bash his head in. He continued to look at me. I'm sure he wished he had a gun so he could blow me away.

I sensed the man was not going to accommodate my request. If his defiance was getting to me, I know it was getting to Rick, and Rick had no qualms about pulling the trigger of the gun he held. Stepping between Rick and the man, into the line of fire, I got in the man's face. I was close enough for him to feel the heat of my breath on his wet, sweaty skin. Spit flew out of my mouth as I screamed at him.

"YOU BETTER GIVE ME YOUR WALLET BEFORE THIS MAN PUTS A SLUG THROUGH YOUR HEAD!"

The man finally broke. He handed me his wallet and I stuffed it into my pocket.

"Now, under the car." I motioned for him and his wife to get underneath their car. The woman jumped down instantly and began crawling on the ground, evening gown and all. The man looked at me like I was crazy.

"GET UNDER THE D— CAR, NOW!"

The man stood defiantly, refusing to move. He had already been robbed. He was not about to succumb to the indignity of crawling on the filthy asphalt in his crisp, shiny tuxedo.

This robbery took a lot longer than planned, and Rick and I were both antsy and tense. Rick wanted to waste this man so we could high tail it outta there. I mustered every fiber of meanness I could exude to get this man under his car.

"GET UNDER THE D— CAR RIGHT NOW, FOOL. IF YOU DON'T WANT THIS SCENE TO TURN UGLY, YOU'D BETTER DO IT NOW!"

The man's expression changed to fear when it registered

that we meant business. He dropped to his hands and knees. Flattening himself out, he half crawled, half rolled underneath the car.

Rick and I jumped into our car, pealing out of the parking lot, leaving behind the burning smell of rubber.

"Whew wee," Rick yelled as I pulled the money out of the wallet and counted it. "How much?"

"Fifty-three bucks," I hollered, waving the bills in the air. "Not bad for two minutes work, huh."

"No kiddin' man. You know," Ronnie continued, "I woulda killed that guy if you hadn't stepped in front of me."

"Yeah, I know."

I'm awed, looking back now, at how God was with me even during that robbery. I know God impressed me to step in front of that man, because if Rick had killed him like he wanted, we'd both be in jail right now serving a life sentence for murder. Most of all, an innocent man would have lost his life so I could have a few moments of pleasure.

— — — — • — — — —

Evelyn kept working and supporting the family. I wouldn't learn, until many, many years later, just how much she had to struggle. I didn't know that her salary wasn't enough to cover all the bills. I didn't know how she had to get a loan from her brother to cover the mortgage so we wouldn't lose the house. I didn't know how many other times she had to beg and borrow just to stay afloat.

What I did know was that Evelyn would keep the home together. And when I felt guilty about my lack of involvement, I reminded myself that she asked for this by insisting on getting a job. This was her fault. If she had just stayed home, things would have been different.

What little money Evelyn had left, she hid from me so I

wouldn't steal it. Eventually, she took my name off our property so I wouldn't get any ideas about taking out a second mortgage, or selling the house.

After awhile, stealing wasn't bringing money in regularly enough for me to keep a constant supply of drugs. All of my buddies, who were single, made most of their money as pimps. Lennie pimped a girl named *Jan, whose sister, *Betsy hung around in our group, getting high with all the rest of us, although she and her children lived on welfare. One day, Lennie offered me a solution for my money woes.

"Yo man, why don't you pimp Betsy?"

"Naw man," I resisted, shaking my head.

"Why not, man? The girl likes you man, and she'd pull some money in for you. You wouldn't have to worry 'bout nothin'. You see what Jan does for me, man. Pays everything."

As the only married man in the group, I'd resisted my friends' previous urges to pimp a woman. The girls expected payment for working, usually sex. Listening to that small inner voice, I couldn't stomach the thought of cheating on Evelyn, although I'd cheated on her already. Each time I did, I broke the most sacred vow of my life, trampling on the last vestiges of my moral ethics. And it still overwhelmed me with guilt.

But I was having trouble satisfying my dope cravings, which was top priority. I saw how the other guys always had the money they needed to buy their drugs. They kept urging me to join the club so I wouldn't have to worry about my cash flow.

I began beating the small voice down. *Evelyn and I may be legally bound,* I thought, *but we have no real marriage. We barely see each other or talk together, let alone have any kind of physical relationship. She can't stand my guts. So, how would I be cheating?*

On and on I rationalized until pimping seemed to be an

okay thing. I finally gave in.

"Yo Betsy," I approached her one night. "You got any money?"

"No, I ain't got no money."

"Well I need some money. Why don't you go on out and make me some money."

It was that simple. Betsy understood what I was asking and she jumped at the chance. She even understood where my boundaries were, knowing I was married and couldn't live with her. The sad thing about it was, I didn't even want to be with her.

Even though I'd rationalized myself into pimping, I never believed it was okay. I despised Betsy. No—I hated her. Every time she walked the streets to find a trick, or each time we had sex, it reminded me of the scum I'd become just to keep my drug habit. Being with Betsy was like picking up a dog from the street and being with it. I hated her for making me hate myself.

But I stayed with her. I gave her what she wanted—a man she could take care of, and she gave me what I needed—money and drugs.

In the drug culture, prostitutes love having a man to take care of. It's a status thing. Each prostitute competes against the others, trying to prove who takes better care of her man.

"Look," one would boast, "my man wears silk suits everyday."

"That ain't nothing," another would say. "My man's driving a Lincoln Continental that I paid for."

It's a sick game of desperation for love and attention. And they have a warped view of what love is.

One night Betsy and I were sitting in my car, a black-on-white, four-door Cadillac sedan. Betsy leaned over on me, putting her arm around my shoulders, our faces a few inches apart.

"Clifford, why don't you ever jump on me?"

"What do you mean?"

"You know, jump on me. Hit me. Beat me up."

"That ain't my thing honey. I don't go around beating up on women."

"But, don't you love me Clifford?"

As stupid and incredible as it sounds, Betsy thought I didn't care about her because I didn't slap her around like other pimps did their women. Pimps were supposed to cuss at their prostitutes, beating them when they got out of line and basically treating them like slaves. Prostitutes expected that treatment. If they weren't handled this way, they questioned whether they were really important to the pimp.

Betsy wanted this show of power and control, but it went against the very grain of my personality. No matter what kind of dirt I did, I never physically hurt another human being. I didn't mind threatening somebody, but I never actually followed through. I couldn't play that part of the prostitution game, though one time I came very close.

My car payment was due and I didn't have the money. The incredible pressure of always needing money crushed me. Sitting in my car with Betsy one day, in the parking lot of a bar where we all hung out, I snapped.

"Gimme some money," I said to Betsy matter of factly.

"I ain't got no money."

"Don't play that s—. I need some money, so gimme some money."

"I'm serious Cliff. I ain't got none."

I knew I sent this girl out and she rarely came back empty handed. I felt she was messing with me, trying to hold out and I wasn't in the mood. Desperate, I determined to get some money from Betsy that day.

"LISTEN B—. I AIN'T PLAYIN' WITH YOU. I GOT TO MAKE MY CAR PAYMENT AND I KNOW YOU GOT SOME MONEY. YOU WORK FOR *ME*, REMEMBER? I KNOW YOU GOT SOME MONEY. SO YOU BETTER GIVE ME SOME D— MONEY."

Betsy paled with fear watching me react in a way she'd never seen. Cowering against the passenger door, she changed her story.

"But Cliff, I got to take care of my children."

"YOU GOT TO WHAT? YOU GOT TO TAKE CARE OF WHO? YOU SUPPOSED TO BE TAKING CARE OF ME."

Jumping out of my car, I ran to the passenger side flinging open the car door. Grabbing Betsy's arm, I yanked her out of the car with such force, she fell to the ground. Screaming and yelling at her, I was totally oblivious to the onlookers standing around in the parking lot.

"YOU WORKIN' FOR ME B—. THAT MONEY YOU MAKE IS FOR ME, TO TAKE CARE OF ME." Crying and shielding herself from my slaps and kicks, Betsy struggled to get up off the ground.

"But I gotta get milk for the baby and the kids need…"

"I DON'T CARE ABOUT YOUR D— KIDS. I GOT BILLS TO PAY. MY CAR NOTE IS OVERDUE. SO YOU BETTER GIT OUT THERE RIGHT NOW AND GET ME SOME MONEY, AND DON'T COME BACK "TIL YOU GOT SOME, *HEAR?*"

Tears streaming down her face, Betsy finally made it to her feet.

"Whattya want me to do?" she sobbed.

"I DON'T GIVE A D— WHAT YOU DO. JUST GIT ME SOME MONEY. GO GIT YOUR WELFARE CHECK IF YOU GOT TO," I said, shoving her hard. She stumbled backwards, fighting for balance.

"But then I won't have any money to get the baby some milk or to pay rent."

"WELL THEN, I GUESS YOU'LL HAVE TO WORK HARDER TONIGHT WON'T YOU?" I turned away and got back in the car. Betsy hurried off to get her welfare check.

My skin crawled as my mind replayed what had just happened. It was the meanest thing I'd ever done to another human being. It was so out of character for me, yet that monster is who I'd become. Chills ran through me as though fingernails had scraped a chalkboard.

When Betsy returned, it was hard for me to even look her in the face. She held out the cash to me. I looked at the money, then looked at her. Seeing the lines of a hard life etched into her skin and tear stains dried on her cheeks, made me want to vomit. Taking the money, we drove off.

Eventually, I cut Betsy off. I hated the person I was becoming. Pimping a human being was not worth the ugliness, the stress, or the guilt. The thought literally came to my mind that pimping my construction tools would be a lot easier and just as lucrative. Maybe, even more so. At least I wouldn't have to scream at them, or slap them around, or have sex with them. Just steal 'em and sell 'em. That, I decided, would become my financial savior.

Do you not know that he who unites himself with a prostitute is one with her in body? For it is said, "The two will become one flesh." But he who unites himself with the Lord is one with Him in spirit.
1 Corinthians 6:16-17

Chapter 9

WIPE OUT

couldn't keep stealing without getting caught, and eventually I did. I spent most of the early 70s in and out of county jails for petty thefts. I hadn't been to jail since my first experience as a teenager, and I still hated the feeling of being confined behind bars. I used every means I could to get out until the trial date.

Usually, I pleaded guilty and got sentenced for 30 days, or 60 days, or maybe even 90 days. Sometimes I only served a third of the time if I behaved good—which I did easily.

Inmates in the county jails stayed in one big room, like a dorm, with rows and rows of cots. Drugs were available to inmates, though not easily accessible. You really had to know someone to score a hit. With no easy access to drugs, I was a virtual choir boy. But the minute I got out, I was devising new schemes for getting my next fix. Obviously, my hatred of jail didn't deter me from stealing, and neither did the physical pain I endured while withdrawing from heroin when I was locked up.

My first experience withdrawing from heroin happened during my first adult stay in jail. Initially, I was only traumatized by the thought of being confined. The longer I sat in my cell, though, the more physically agitated I became.

Soon, I paced the cell, back and forth, back and forth. My body wouldn't allow me to sit still. I wiped my nose constantly with my hand, or my clothes, or the sheets, as fluid dripped from my nostrils.

As more time passed, sharp knives ripped my muscles as cramp spasms shot through me. Unable to stand, I doubled over, curling my long frame into a ball as if to condense the amount of space available for the pain to travel through.

Hot flashes drenched me in sweat that mingled with the spit trickling from either side of my mouth. Then just as quickly, I shook uncontrollably with violent chills as cold flashes took the reins.

Racked with pain, I couldn't sleep or eat. I endured this intense cleansing of poison from my system for four or five days before I felt any inkling of relief. After about two weeks, the withdrawal ended.

When I left jail, I left with my insides as pure as gold burnished by fire. Like the whiteness of a fresh snowfall. So pure, that the next heroin high I got was almost as good as the very first time I tried it. Powerful—because it had a clean, straight shot to my nervous system. Still, it wasn't quite the same high.

Later, back in jail, I discovered I didn't have to go through heroin withdrawal "cold turkey." Lots of inmates took methadone—a synthetic drug that blocks the gaps made from the lack of heroin, so that the withdrawal symptoms aren't so bad. But that didn't make sense to me, because methadone was addicting too. Why trade one addiction for another?

Besides, I enjoyed the highs I got after being cleaned out. Perversely, I would think about how great my next high was going to be, while in the throes of withdrawal. Anxiously awaiting the opportunity to get back out on the street to get my next fix.

————•————

Without warning, the boundaries I so diligently etched between my personal life and family life melded, the lines of distinction blurring into one sad picture. The deeper I walked into the depths of drug addiction, the more I relinquished my ability to rationally control my behavior.

Blinded by complete denial, I thought I was keeping my drug use a secret from my family. Several times, Evelyn found burnt spoons and syringes in the house, and accused me of using. Each time I adamantly denied it.

"Please Cliff," she begged once, "please get help. If you do, I'll stand by you. I'll be here for you. Just get some help."

"Whatta you talkin' about? I told you I ain't usin' no drugs."

"That's okay Clifford, you don't have to pretend with me. I know you're using, and I just want you to get some help. They're ruining your life. Look at you! Look at us!"

Furious, I stomped out the house in search of a fresh hit, just to calm myself down. Never, did I admit to Evelyn that I used drugs. Gradually her accusations stopped.

One day one of my street friends shoved a handful of pills at me.

"Hey Cliff, you should try these man." Looking at the mound in his hand, I asked him what they were.

"Oh man, just take 'em. I promise, man, they'll get you real high."

"How much you selling 'em for?"

He gave a little chuckle, playfully slapping my shoulder. "Nothin', man, nothin'. This batch is on me. If you like 'em and want some more, you know where to find me."
Always glad for freebies, I swallowed all of them.

Sometime after I'd returned home, I had some kind of reaction to those pills. I woke up to find my sons, Stephen and Jeffrey, on either side of me, their slight bodies straining to keep my six-foot two-inch frame from tumbling over.

"Hold him up, Stephen," I heard Jeffrey yelling through my

stupor, his voice urgently concerned. "Don't let him fall. Don't let him fall and hurt himself."

With every fiber of might they could muster, Stephen and Jeffrey struggled with me, their breath heaving fast and heavy as they maneuvered me to the couch. They let me drop into the safety of the cushions.

I knew it wasn't right—my sons having to see their father like this. I wanted them to just go away, and turn their faces from the sight of me. But as if pampering a wounded animal, my sons sat with me on the couch, not wanting to walk away without making sure I was okay.

A rational person would have seen the red flag from that experience. But I wasn't rational. Years later, as Stephen recalled those days, he shared with me how he remembered the smell of heroin cooking, as I sat in the bathroom preparing to shoot up.

"Daddy, that smell was so strong, it filled the whole house," he said. Then he shared how he'd go in the bathroom after I'd left, and open the windows and spray air freshener because he didn't want his Mama to come home to that smell.

The more my street life blended with my family life, the worse we all became. No one really talked to anyone else. Evelyn came home, went to her bedroom and shut the door, and each of the kids did the same.

Evelyn, Stephen and Rhonda stopped going to church, embarrassed by everyone's common knowledge of my drug addiction. But that didn't stop Jeffrey from going, though.

Every time I saw Jeffrey head for church, I'd think to myself *I should be walking beside him. I should be taking him, and Stephen and Rhonda to church.* Then I'd promise myself, for the millionth time, that I was going to change. Get out of this drug habit and be a real father to my kids. I was going to do it.

As soon as I was strong enough to fight. Maybe tomorrow.

Evelyn and I established an uneasy truce. She didn't speak much to me and I stayed away from her. Though every once in a while, between our really bad spells, she tried to persuade me to participate in some family activity. One summer, sensing a vital need for family togetherness, Evelyn began planning a vacation trip.

"I thought it would be nice to take the kids on a special vacation, just to get away for a few days," Evelyn informed me one day. "I was thinking, maybe we could go to the Black Hills in South Dakota. Take them to see the presidents' faces carved in the stone, and stuff."

Evelyn talked excitedly about the trip. I'm sure the opportunity to leave the craziness of our life behind and relax made her ecstatic. It was the first time in a long time I saw her so happily animated.

"Hey, why don't you come with us Cliff?"

I rolled my eyes and spat out, "Ain't nothin' I want to see up in them Black Hills."

Evelyn ignored my gruff attitude, choosing not to have her good mood dampened.

"Oh come on Cliff, it'll be fun. Just the five of us on a real family vacation. The kids would absolutely love it. And I would too, really. I want you to go with us. Please?"

And do what, I thought to myself. *Weren't no drugs up in them Black Hills.* I looked at Evelyn's pleading face, the yearning in her eyes speaking volumes about her feelings. I believed her when she said she really wanted me to go. I felt a pang of sensitivity, but it didn't change my mind.

All during the days and days of planning, Evelyn and the kids pressured me to come with them. Each time I shook my head no, refusing their invitation. But that didn't deter them.

Even in the final days, when they were packing their suitcases, they still begged me to come along.

"Come on daddy, you can put your clothes in with mine," Rhonda kept saying. It seemed to take forever before their leaving day finally arrived. I was anxious for my next fix and I really wanted them to leave.

With the suitcases and kids packed in the car, Evelyn made one final attempt.

"Clifford, you sure you don't want to go? We really want you..."

"Dang, Evelyn. How many times I got to say no? I AIN'T GOIN' WITH YOU! Now don't ask me again."

As the words roared from my mouth, I knew the harshness was unnecessary. After all the crap I'd put Evelyn through, she had laid that aside and reached out to me. But I couldn't seem to stop the evilness from erupting. Drugs had changed my whole personality.

Evelyn stared at me, hurt flooding her eyes. Shaking her head, the tears overflowed her cheeks as she started to cry. Without another word, she got in the car, closing the door. As the car drove off, kids waving at me with depressed-looking faces, I thought, how great it was going to be with the family gone for a whole week. I'd be able to cop a lot of highs, without any hassle.

The car was barely out of sight before I raced into the house on a search mission. Evelyn controlled all the money, employing elaborate methods to hide it from me. Somehow, when she was home, she'd found a way to keep her pocketbook out of my sight. Sometimes at night, she slept with her cash in her bra.

Methodically, I went from room to room in the house. I turned over the chair and couch cushions and rummaged through all the drawers and closets. I pulled out clothes, boxes of shoes and purses, leaving everything strewn around behind me. I was a human tornado, snaking a deadly path through the house.

As the minutes ticked by, I became more frantic. I needed money to ease the incessant yearning in my gut. There had to be something, somewhere. It took me nearly one hour before I hit the jackpot. The checkbook! I found the checkbook, hidden deep in the back of Evelyn's closet.

HAH! I thought. *You can't fool ol' Clifford.*

Checkbook in hand I headed for the bank. Asking for the balance, I withdrew $40 or $50 to buy my drug stash. I did this everyday—sometimes twice a day—until the bank account was completely empty.

Walking away with the last of the money in hand, it hit me what I had done. I couldn't believe I cleaned out over $500 from that account, all spent financing my drug habit. Why did I do that? How was I going to explain that to Evelyn? What was she going to do? She had no more money.

I'll just replace it. I'll get a good fix, and then steal something to pawn. I'll put the money back in and she'll never miss it. Yeah!

But in the back of my head, I knew I was just lying to myself as usual. I'd never replace the money.

It wasn't until the day after Evelyn and the kids got back in town, that she went to the bank. I just happened to be home when she walked in. The front door cracking against the frame announced her return.

THUD! Evelyn's purse landed in the chair, after sailing through the air. Undefiled hatred clouded her face and eyes. Her voice dripped with venom.

"Clifford. How could you do that? HOW COULD YOU DO THAT?" she screamed.

"How could I do WHAT?"

"I can't believe you could be this cold-blooded. This heartless. You are not the same caring man I married."

"WHAT."

"HOW COULD YOU TAKE ALL MY MONEY? HOW COULD YOU TAKE ALL MY MONEY?"

Evelyn's uncontrollable sobbing punctuated her words. How was she going to pay the phone bill or the house note? Do I know how much money she'd spent for the vacation? How was she going to buy food for the kids?

"HOW COULD YOU DO THAT CLIFFORD?"

Shrugging my shoulders, I sat on the nearest chair. I mustered every ounce of humbleness I could find.

"I'm sorry."

"DON'T tell me you're SORRY. I'VE HEARD THAT A MILLION TIMES. DON'T TELL ME YOU'RE SORRY! YOU'RE NOT SORRY, CLIFFORD. YOU'RE NOT SORRY, 'CAUSE YOU DON'T CARE. YOU DON'T CARE ABOUT ME. YOU DON'T CARE ABOUT THE KIDS. YOU DON'T CARE BECAUSE YOU DON'T LOVE US ANYMORE, CLIFFORD. IF YOU LOVED US, YOU WOULDN'T HURT ME AND THE CHILDREN THIS WAY! IF YOU LOVED US, YOU'D CHANGE."

Broken, exasperated, and defeated, Evelyn looked like a neglected, wilted flower. I had nothing to say to make her feel any differently than how she felt at that moment. To her, I was lower than scum. Lower than mildew on the bathroom tile. Lower than slime on the ocean's floor.

I retreated to the basement until she cooled off. Those accusing voices went off like screaming sirens in my head. I WAS scum, and everything else she'd ever called me. Only scum would take the food out of a baby's mouth and sell it for drugs.

Evelyn's and my relationship ended at that point. She didn't care about my coming or going. She did her thing and she let me do my thing, without any questions or comments. Evelyn and the kids, and me, just existed—carrying on our lives independent of each other, as though we were strangers passing in the night.

————•————

I continued to spend every waking moment figuring out how to steal or con people for money. That was my full-time job. Other people got up and went to work in buildings, I got up and went to work in the streets. Drugs inspired me with confidence, making me stupidly bold.

Pawn brokers loved the construction stuff I stole, particularly the power tools, because they resold quickly. Sometimes, I stole tools from one construction site and sold them cheap at another construction site.

Once, I went to a site and decided to steal an arc-welder—an electrical box tool the size of a very large stereo speaker. But it was too heavy for me to lift.

"Hey buddy," I called to a welder standing some 20 feet away. "Hey man, why don't you come on over and help me with this thing?"

The man walked over and grabbed one end. "Yeah, thanks man, " I said, launching into this whole made-up story. "I don't know where Tom is. He's supposed to be comin' around the corner to help me with this thing."

We lifted the arc welder and walked it through the gate surrounding the construction site. Heaving it into my truck, I thanked the man for his help. "Oh," I added, "when you see that d— idiot, Tom, cuss him out for me."

Another time, I saw a guy I knew, a contractor who had

bought stolen tools from me before, standing in front of his new construction site—a house he was building.

"What's up guy," I greeted him, extending my hand and shaking his. We chatted for a minute.

"Hey look, I can get you a whole truckload of two-by-fours and plywood. Interested?"

"How much you want for it?"

"Well, let's see. I'll have to pay up front to rent a truck, and pay somebody else, up front, to help me load it. Gimme $500 for the whole deal."

"Okay, but I'll have to give it to you when I get the stuff."

"No, I gotta have the money now."

The guy didn't have any money on him, so I followed him in my car as he drove to the bank. Handing me the $500, he shook my hand.

"Alright now, I'll see you in two days with the stuff." I drove off, waving and smiling. I didn't have any two-by-fours or plywood for the guy, but he didn't know that. He believed my story because he didn't have any reason not to, since we'd done business together before.

For two days I didn't have to hustle so hard. And I could have left it at that. But I didn't. Another idea came to me. On the third day, I went back to see the same man. As I walked up to him, I noticed he acted a little perturbed.

"Hey man, what the h— happened to you? And where's my stuff?"

"Look man, I'm sorry, but when I went to the job to get the wood, the police came, man. I had to put the stuff back, man, you know how it is. It was just bad timing. But if you want me to, I'll try it again."

"Yeah I want you to try it again."

Sniffing and scratching my nose, I said, "yeah well, you

know man I had to rent that truck and everything, so, you know, if you want me to try it again, you'll have to give me another $500."

The guy paused a minute, pondering my offer. I kept talking, trying to help him make up his mind.

"I'm sure I can get it this time, man. The police ain't gonna come to the same place, so it shouldn't be a problem."

Finally, the man agreed and gave me another $500. I drove away, smiling and waving, laughing inside. *"D— Clifford,"* I said to myself, *"you're good."*

I didn't reserve my con stories just for people on the street. I conned whoever I could in order to get money for drugs. Including my family.

Daddy had long since retired from the construction business, and he and mama moved back to Florida to live out their golden years. They were completely aware of my drug addiction and their inability to help me.

On this particular day, I needed a fix in the worst way, and was frantically trying to scheme my way to some money. I didn't have anybody who could give me any, and couldn't think of anything to steal. I couldn't even think clearly enough to come up with any schemes. I was getting desperate.

I thought about mama and daddy in Florida. Maybe I could call them with a hard-luck story, so sad, that even they would be compelled to send me money. It had to be perfectly convincing—daddy was used to my con games and was not an easy sell.

"Daddy, I really need your help," I began immediately. I made my voice sound as pathetic as possible. I didn't waste time with greetings and frivolous conversation. I had to sound urgent.

"What's the matter, Clifford?"

"I'm really in trouble daddy. We've gotten behind in our mortgage payments and we've been trying to catch up, but they're saying they're gonna repossess the house if we don't pay the money we owe, TODAY."

Daddy silently listened as I explained the situation. Evelyn's been working so hard, and I've been trying so hard, but we just haven't been able to pull it off. It's not like the last time when we just had Stephen and he was a baby, but now we've got three kids, and what are we gonna do if they throw us out on the street...

"How much you need, Cliff?"

"A thousand dollars, daddy."

My father didn't just fall into the con. Through the phone, I could feel him weighing my story. If it was fake and he gave me the money, he'd be out of some serious cash. If it was true and he didn't give me the money, his son, his grandchildren and his daughter-in-law would be out on the street.

"Please daddy."

He knew I was messed up, but I was still his son and he was still my daddy.

"Well Clifford, if I send you this money are you gonna pay me..."

"Yes, yes daddy. I will pay you back every cent of the money just as soon as I can. I'm starting a new job in Littleton next week, but if I don't pay the money by 6:00 TODAY, we will lose the house, and I can't let that happen. I just can't."

With a heavy sigh that reeked of questioning his own judgement, daddy said, "Alright. I'll wire you the money." I thanked him profusely, repeating how I was gonna pay him back, thanking him for bailing me out, yet again.

Hanging up the phone, I began dreaming of all the drugs I was gonna buy with that $1,000. Once I got the money, I put every cent into my arm.

————•————

The end of my family life, as I'd known it, came abruptly.

Rushing home one day, I raced through the front door and headed for the basement. I had just copped some heroin and rushed to satisfy my craving. Oblivious to anything other than the relief waiting for me in the coming "high," I proceeded to cook up a little batch.

I went through the routine, tingling with expectation. Just as I slid the needle into my vein, but before I could push the liquid through, I heard footsteps descending the stairs.

Startled, my head whipped toward the sound and my eyes settled on twelve-year-old Stephen making his way down into the basement, to his bedroom. Exposed, I froze—unable to move or speak as I listened to each foot slap the tiled steps. With each sound, my heart thumped a little louder.

When Stephen's innocent face came into view, I watched his eyes leave my gaze and travel down my arm, feeling their heat burning a hole in my skin. I became acutely aware of the syringe protruding from my vein, anchored by the needle still inside, my thumb resting on the plunger.

Stephen stopped on the next to the last stair, making him eye level with me. I felt naked, trying not to shiver from the cold blast of shame that threatened to overtake me. Here was Stephen—standing on the brink of his own transformation into manhood—gazing on his hero. What a shining example of a wasted man I displayed, a stocking wrapped around his arm, needle dangling from his flesh, the stench of drugs cutting the air.

With glassy eyes brimming at the edge, Stephen pointed his skinny finger at me. "Daddy, that's what you went to jail for last week."

131

Without another word, Stephen walked past me into his bedroom, leaving his shredded innocence heaped at my feet. The slammed door screamed his anger, shutting off the light's glow, releasing me to the cloak of darkness.

Shame, then guilt, stabbed my heart. My head ached as I relived over and over what just happened. What have I done? How could I ever face my child again? He knew the truth first-hand—having stood boldly in its ugliness, unprotected.

My insides screamed and groaned, and cried for my children, my family, and myself. Slowly I pushed the plunger down, flooding my arm with my savior, my drug, my escape. All the while, I knew it was time to go. If the only thing I could give this family was the ugliness Stephen had just seen, I didn't need to be here anymore.

That night I packed a bag and left home.

Evelyn divorced me later that year. Completely severed from my family, I fell off the deep end. I may have thought I'd already hit bottom, but I didn't even know what bottom was until I was completely alone.

Do not be deceived:
God cannot be mocked.
A man reaps what he sows.
Galatians 6:7

Chapter 10

SYNACORE

I left my home with an I-don't-need-you attitude, as if I acted like I needed my family all along. The only thing that ripped my heart was leaving my children.

I rented an old house right down the street from my sister. A cot served as the one piece of furniture in the entire house. Rats were my roommates. The house pulsated with them as they ran all over the place. At night, they squeaked mouse conversations to each other, while their feet pitter-pattered across the room.

Now that I was a free man, one might think I was elated at the prospect of being able to run with my friends and drug partners without getting any hassle from home. Truth is, I stopped hanging out with my friends completely. I retreated into myself, becoming a loner.

My one all-consuming thought was getting my next fix. Not working, money was ALWAYS the primary issue. I stole heavily from construction sites, reselling my loot on the street to finance my addiction.

About a week after moving away from Evelyn and the family, I hit a construction site in broad daylight, filling my old truck with a bunch of stuff. Once I got rid of that load, instead of going to a different construction site, I went right back to the same site for some more stuff. Of course people were watching me and called the police, who busted me. I went right to jail.

When I wasn't stealing, I found other ways to get drugs. Naturally, I knew all the drug dealers around Denver, and they knew me. Sometimes, depending upon how well I knew a dealer, my incessant begging persuaded one to give me drugs on credit, with my promise to pay later. When that didn't work, I schemed other ways of getting what I needed. In one foolishly bold instance, I even stole from a dealer.

Peter, or Pete as we called him, was a well-known drug dealer whose house received a heavy volume of visitors, including me. Constant foot traffic flowed to and from his residence. Each time I went to Pete's house to buy drugs, he did the same thing—he'd leave me standing in the house, go out the back door, then return with the goods.

In one of my desperate-for-drugs-but-broke states, I paid Pete a secret visit. I'd thought about his ritual and decided to stake out his place. Driving to his house, I didn't do my usual—park the car and go inside Pete's house. Oh no. On this day, I parked my car around the corner, to give me a clear view of the back of Pete's house.

I didn't have long to wait before I saw Pete come out the back door and walk to his basement. In those days, the old houses' basements were accessed from outside. Watching the basement door, I saw Pete emerge holding something in his hand. Pete sauntered back into the house, and I discovered the jackpot. Obviously, Pete hid his drug stash in the basement. All I had to do was find out where, and I was home free.

The minute Pete disappeared into his house, I got out of my car and swiftly headed to Pete's backyard. It didn't matter that it was broad daylight and Pete, or anyone, could have seen me. I fixed my mind on one goal and one goal only—getting the drugs I craved.

Carefully, I ducked the windows and doors, moving quickly

and silently, eyes peeling this way and that, hoping no one was watching. Once at the basement door, I opened it and swiftly descended the stairs. It took a few seconds for my eyes to adjust to the darkness before I made out anything in the room. With no idea where to begin searching for Pete's drug stash, I couldn't take long to ponder. It seems like no sooner that I got into the basement, I heard footsteps. The basement door opened, daylight flooding the stairs.

Frantically, I searched for a hiding place. Pete, a typical drug dealer, didn't mess around when it came to business. He packed a weapon and wouldn't hesitate to blow me away if he found me in his house.

Hearing the shoes click on the stairs, I burrowed deep into the shadows as Pete's form came into view. Holding my breath, I hoped the sound of my beating heart wasn't as loud as it seemed to me.

Pete went into one of the basement rooms, then came out holding a bag of drugs. Never sensing my presence, he went back up the stairs, leaving me with the valuable clue. Making certain Pete was gone, I went to the room and found the goldmine. Hidden above the furnace was Pete's entire drug stash.

I stuffed it all into my pockets, excitedly anticipating the fix awaiting me. Adrenaline pumping, I scurried out of the basement back to my car and took off, never looking back.

Eventually, I crossed the other side of the fence, becoming a dealer myself. I began working for George, a dealer, who I knew very well, who'd gotten tired of giving me freebies.

"Aw come on George," I pleaded. "Just give me a small dose, man. You know I'm good for it."

Shaking his head, George said no. He was tired of me begging him to trust me to pay him for the stash later. He knew he couldn't trust me as far as he could spit.

"But here's what I'll do," he countered. All ears, I eagerly waited for his suggestion, ready to do anything to quiet my body. "I'll let you deal for me on the streets and you can earn your heroin that way."

"Sure man, whatever." With those three little words, I became a drug dealer.

George measured the heroin and put it in small, rubber balloons, tying the ends. These balloons are what I sold on the street. "If you think the cops are on to you," George schooled me, "you swallow the evidence."

And that's what I did. On several occasions, I swallowed those balloons when the cops got too close. With extreme control, I kept myself from gagging while the muscles worked those rubber blobs down my throat. My stomach bloated from all that foreign mass invading my body. A bowel movement provided the only opportunity to retrieve the balloons. After defecating, I dug my bare hands into my own feces, picking it apart to recover the balloons, still intact.

If any of those balloons had burst, I probably would have died from all the heroin exploding into my system. But at that time, thoughts like that never entered my mind. All I knew was I made enough money to support my habit and I wasn't about to get caught doing it, though I had a couple of close calls.

Standing on a corner in front of a bar one day, I guarded about five or six balloons stuffed in my pocket. The rest of my supply lay hidden behind some buildings across the street. Waiting for potential customers, I spotted a car slowly moving down the street. As it turned the corner, one of the four men in the car looked right into my eyes.

Instinctively I knew it was an unmarked police car and they were coming for me. As they parked the car, I coolly sauntered into the bar walking toward the men's restroom, but ducking out a side door. Fighting the urge to run, I calmly walked across the street to my parked car and got inside.

Driving the car from the curb, I watched the cops through my rearview mirror. They came out of the bar's front door, stood on the sidewalk, and searched up and down the street for me. I smiled smugly, gloating at how I'd outsmarted them.

I later learned that someone had "dropped a dime" on me—meaning they had fingered me to the cops as a drug dealer. Though I wasn't caught that time, I knew they wouldn't stop until they did. I really had to keep my eyes open.

Though I never got busted for dealing heroin, no such luck allowed me to keep using without ever getting busted for possession of heroin. When it finally happened, it wasn't a 30-day or 60-day jail sentence, but a one-year sentence. A whole year! I couldn't stand the thought of being locked behind bars for an entire year.

Depression overwhelmed me, and this time I couldn't scheme up a way of escape . I faced my predicament head on, and it absolutely freaked me out. I had to find some way to get out because I knew I wouldn't survive a whole year in jail. The answer to my problem fell right into my lap.

Talking with a jail inmate one day, he mentioned Synacore.

"What the h— is Synacore?"

"You ain't heard of Synacore, man?"

"Naw."

As it turned out, Synacore was a privately-owned drug rehab facility run by the husband-wife team of Luke and Dottie. Based in California, Synacore was the darling rehab program of the nation in the 1970s—even garnering a nod from Hollywood where a movie was made about its work. With two facilities, one in Denver and the other in Long Beach,

Synacore was the "great white hope" for anyone who had drug problems.

The best part about the program was, if accepted, I would be released from jail and allowed to serve my time at Synacore. This was music to my ears, and I set about planning my best con scheme to get accepted into the facility. Ready to put on my best performance, I dialed the number.

"Synacore, may I help you?" The voice on the other end was pleasant and soothing.

"Uh, hi. My name is Clifford Harris, and somebody told me about your program. I just wanted to get some more information about it."

"Are you calling for yourself or someone else?"

"Uh, no—I'm calling for myself."

"Hold on, and I'll get you one of the counselors."

When the counselor got on the phone, I poured it on thick and heavy. My voice dripped with as much despair and contriteness as I could muster. I talked about how disgusting my drug habit was, how they had ruined my life, and how badly I wanted to change. By the time I finished, I had an appointment for an interview. Synacore sent one of their counselors, a man, to the jail to talk with me. I reached out my hand, with a look of utter relief, and enthusiastically shook his.

"I'm really glad to meet you Clifford. We're always anxious to talk with someone who asks for help."

"Well, Lord knows I really need it," I confirmed, briskly nodding my head. "My life is such a mess, I mean, I sure wouldn't be in here if it wasn't."

"How long have you been a drug addict, Clifford?"

I launched into the entire story, not hesitating to include each sordid detail. Granted, I had definitely messed up my life, but I made it sound as gruesome as possible. All the while, coming across like I desperately wanted help. Honestly, I don't even know if I really was asking for help. I'd gone into this as a con to get out of jail. Who knows, I may have been conning myself as well.

The counselor listened intently, stopping me every now and then to ask questions. While I talked, I could tell by his face he was ready to sign me up immediately. When I'd answered everything to his satisfaction, the counselor took the lead.

"Well Clifford, it sounds like Synacore can definitely help you, but you need to know that it's not a picnic. Don't think you can leave jail, and that's it. We mean business. We have a very strict program, and you need to understand that. It's imperative that you obey the rules, or you will be out of the program."

"Yes sir," I gushed. "Oh, I understand perfectly. And I don't care how hard it is, I just want help to beat this habit."

Before the end of the week, the jail transferred me to Synacore.

— — — —•— — — —

Once at Synacore, I finally met the infamous Luke and Dottie. Luke was a big, tall man with a gruff voice. Dottie was a skinny woman, with red hair.

Synacore was a co-ed facility— and the counselor wasn't kidding—operated by very strict rules. There were about 50 or 60 residents living there. I already knew many of the Blacks in the facility. One of the residents, Buck—an older man in his fifties—and I used to get high on the streets together.

Buck and I entered a contract, meaning we watched each other's back. With Buck's help, it didn't take me long to figure out the Synacore system. I used Buck to get ahead and he used me. It wasn't long before we beat Luke and Dottie at their own game.

Humiliation was the number one tactic used to control behavior. If a woman resident broke a rule, she wasn't allowed to wear make-up, or they would make her wear baggy pants or an oversized man's shirt to make her look bummy. If it was a guy, they would make him shave his head, or maybe wear a diaper.

Then, they would make the offender sit in front of all the other residents, and proceed to talk about him or her like a dog. They really liked it when other residents chimed in with something to say, because that added to the humiliation.

One night, a little after 2:00 a.m., I heard voices yelling in the hall.

"HOUSE MEETING DOWNSTAIRS. HOUSE MEETING DOWNSTAIRS."

Somebody came into my room, and started shaking me.

"Hey, Clifford, wake up. Come on, we've got a house meeting."

"Yeah yeah, alright."

Herded into the main room, all the residents sat in chairs formed in a semi-circle, taking up three-fourths of the room. At the open end of the circle sat the house manager, his eyes pinned to the floor. Luke stood as the accuser.

"You can all thank this man as the reason for being brutally aroused from your sleep. You know, Dottie and I believe it's important to reward you when you demonstrate trustworthiness and dedication. We like to see residents take more responsibility as you prove you can handle it. But when you abuse our trust—when you abuse your position, we cannot allow that."

The house manager was a resident of the program who had proven himself to Luke and Dottie, and had worked his way up to that position. He basically ran the facility, allowing him a lot more freedom than the other residents.

Luke had just found the guy in the basement, having sex with one of the other residents. While Luke ranted and raved about how the guy had cheated and lied, and violated their trust and taken advantage of his position, I sensed a great opportunity. When Luke paused, I raised my hand.

"Yes, Clifford?"

"Yeah, uh, I knew somethin' was goin' on between them two, cause they used to sneak around too much. I spotted them a couple of times coming from the basement, acting all weird and stuff..."

I had no idea what I was talking about because I had never seen anything. But I knew Luke would appreciate me backing him up, so I kept on going.

"But, you know, I couldn't report them cause I never SAW anything wrong. But I used to see them downstairs and it made me wonder, you know."

Boy, did Luke jump on my tip then. He was so transparent. All anyone had to do was praise him or the program, or back him up and he was ready to promote their butts right on up the ladder. With that in mind, in any house meeting, I made it a habit to say something to the group, like "Come on, we need to listen up," or "they're just trying to straighten us out"— anything that showed I was on their side.

One day, out of the blue, I was summoned to the office.

"Clifford, we're transferring you to our Synacore facility in Long Beach, California," Luke informed me.

"What? Why?"

Luke tried to make up some excuse that sounded reasonable and good, but the change was too sudden. When I told Buck, I got the real reason. Apparently, my sister, Melba, had come to Synacore asking to see me. Synacore did not allow family visits, ever. So to keep my family away, they decided to transfer me.

The Long Beach facility was a refurbished six-story building that used to be a theater. In fact, it still housed a theater, and a ballroom. All the women stayed on one floor, and all the men stayed on the top floor. There were no individual rooms. Just one big room with beds on either side of it, like army barracks. And if I thought Denver's facility was strict, this one was worse.

I continued to please Luke and Dottie in every way I could, watching them lap it up like doggie treats. To them I was their prize user—a gruesome, hard-luck story of a man whose life had gone down the toilet due to drugs, on the way to being totally reformed and rehabilitated by the Synacore program. And my being a Black man was icing on the cake for them.

They used my picture to generate the positive publicity that encouraged donations of support from individuals and corporations, and state-funded grants. Everybody loved Synacore, and donors never passed up an opportunity to let us residents know how much we owed Luke and Dottie, and how grateful we should be that they cared so much.

Sometimes they even said stuff like "If Luke and Dottie told me to lie down in the middle of the street, I'd do it. I wouldn't even hesitate, because I have so much faith in them."

Well I didn't, but I kept that to myself. I just smiled at the right times for the pictures, and did what I was told without arguing or causing problems. I didn't mind them using me one bit, because I was using them to work my way up to house manager.

At daily group sessions, Luke and Dottie often played something they called "The Game." If a resident or employee had a problem with another resident, he or she wrote a note, signed his or her name, and dropped it into a special box. Then the two of them faced off in front of the entire group.

During the face off, the leaders always tried to goad the resident, with whom the other had the problem, into a yelling or screaming reaction. The leaders really seemed to get off on trying to provoke an emotional response. A couple of times someone put my name in the box and I had to "play", but I always kept my composure. I think this irritated some people, especially Roger.

Roger was a former resident of Synacore who graduated from the program, then came back to the facility to work as a counselor. One morning, Roger called me to his office.

"What's up?" I asked, wondering what Roger needed me for.

"I need you to follow me," he said, leading me downstairs to the theater level of the building. We stopped in a large, very clean bathroom. It had about ten urinals and eight stalls.

"I want you to clean this bathroom."

"Yes sir." No argument. No protest.

"Here are the cleaning supplies and the mop. When you're done, come back to my office and I'll return to check your work."

"No problem, Roger."

About an hour later, I stood up to survey my work. I had worked hard—cleaning the toilets and urinals with a rag, my hands immersed in the water; cleaning the counter tops, the sinks, the tiles, mopping the floor. I even dusted the tops of the stalls. The bathroom was spotless. Satisfied, I went to Roger's office to let him know I was finished.

When he came to the bathroom, Roger walked through the immense room, surveying my work. When he was done, he looked at me and simply said, "Clean it again."

"Okay," I said, matching his nonchalance.

I already had Roger figured out. He was trying to provoke some kind of angry reaction, and it wasn't gonna happen. *Ain't no way you gonna beat THIS con man*, I thought to myself as I started repeating what I had just done. "I got all the time in the world and no where to go." I smiled like the cheshire cat who ate the canary.

When Roger came back the second time, he checked my work again, then said, "Do it again."

"Yes sir," I responded, as serenely and pleasantly as possible, all the while laughing hysterically inside my head. Did this fool really think he was gonna make me blink? If he wanted me to clean the bathroom twenty times, I was going to do it. Like I said, where did I have to go?

So for the third time, I cleaned every inch of that bathroom the same way I had done twice before. Finished, I called Roger down. After he walked through this time, he stood in front of me.

"Fine job." Then he turned and walked away.

The next time The Game was played in group, someone called my name. I sat in the center of the room. And who should come walking up, but Roger.

"In case you wondered about that episode with the bathroom, I admit I tried to make you angry."

I feigned surprise. "Is THAT what you were doing? I just thought I hadn't cleaned something good enough, which is why I did it over again."

Now it was Roger's turn to be surprised, though his was genuine.

"Really?

I stifled a laugh. "Oh, yes sir. I thought you saw something that made you think I was trying to sneak, so I made sure to do it all over again."

"Now see," Roger turned to everybody else, "Clifford here did exactly what we're trying to teach you. You have to learn to trust us, even if the lessons are hard on you. But if you do what we say, like Clifford, you'll get along just fine at Synacore."

Turning back to me, Roger squeezed my shoulder with approval. "You did fine."

"Thank you, sir." I grinned a full-mouth smile. This had been too easy. All I did was act like the idiot they believed we all were.

Within a few weeks, I was promoted to house manager for the men.

————•————

Synacore bought a restaurant in Anaheim, near Disneyland, and Luke and Dottie made all the addicts work there. That was the only time any Synacore residents were allowed outside the facility.

I started as a bus boy, eventually working my way to waiter. I got along great with the customers—since I'm such a people person—and soon they nicknamed me Mr. Hospitality.

After four months in the program, I was Luke and Dottie's model of success—one of Luke's guys. But I hadn't changed. Being at Synacore was kept me out of jail, but being at Synacore did not repress my desire for drugs. I often day-dreamed of what it would feel like to get my hands on some drugs. I basked in imagined sensations of a good high.

Between the restaurant and the two facilities, Luke and Dottie made money hand-over-fist. They bought food in bulk, and received huge price breaks because of the program. Meanwhile, their clothes got flashier, and the cars got bigger and more luxurious. Finally, Luke announced he'd decided to become a country-western singer. He bought a big tour bus, and traveled around.

I kept kissing their butts whenever I had the chance, ratting on anyone I saw cheating or breaking the rules. I was rewarded by being promoted to a cashier. As the trusted cash register operator, I decided to start a little nest egg so I could have some money when I got out of the program. I figured if I stole one dollar a day, they'd never miss it.

I couldn't risk hiding the money in my room, due to the periodic searches Synacore counselors engaged in. I found other ways to stash the cash, creating hiding places throughout the building. I hid money all over the facility—in the girl's bathroom, in the basement, under rugs, and behind the theater stage.

Of course my kiss-up tactics spawned many enemies. As long as Luke and Dottie were around, I had it good. The minute they left town for vacation or a singing gig, I was at the mercy of the people left in charge. At the restaurant, it was Frank. And Frank reeked with jealousy toward me. Numerous times I'd heard him whisper through his teeth "I'm gonna take you down, Mr. Hospitality."

Frank got his chance to mess with me when Luke and Dottie went on a trip that lasted several weeks. He'd waited a long time, as I was in my eleventh month at Synacore. One month shy of finishing my year-long sentence.

"Clifford, I've got a new job for you." If Frank had gloated any more he would have burst a gut like a balloon too full of air.

"Yeah, what's that?"

"I need another cook in the kitchen, and since you're such a GOOD worker, I'm going to give that job to you."

"Uh, no you're not, cause I ain't doin' it."

"Uh, I think you are."

"NO, I think I'm not! I ain't gonna be no COOK." Throwing an arm around my shoulder, Frank looked at me like I was a naughty child.

"Come on, why don't we talk about it"

"Ain't nothin' to talk about," I said, shrugging his arm off my shoulder. "I AIN'T goin' in that kitchen, period! In fact, I'm not doin' nothin' else around here. I'm LEAVING."

Without another word, I turned and left Frank standing with a gaping mouth. While no one was looking, I retrieved all my hidden dollars and left the restaurant.

Back in my room, I got my clothes and stuffed them into a brown paper bag. I don't know why I'd decided to buck the system. Maybe all that kissing up had finally sickened me. Maybe I was tired of playing games. Maybe I got too cocky, thinking they wouldn't do anything to me if I stood up to them.

Getting my clothes and money together, I thought about other residents who'd walked out of the program. The leaders always denigrated them to those of us left behind, saying stuff like "he really didn't want to change," or "she just couldn't cut it." They made snide comments about what losers those residents were, sneaking out the back door in the middle of the night, not even having the guts to walk out the front door and let everyone know they were leaving.

Well, nobody was going to say that about Clifford. I picked up my grocery bag and walked right to the front desk.

"I'm leaving." I smiled at the man sitting there, and proceeded through the FRONT door, even pausing to turn around and wave at him.

With $30 of stolen cash-register money and my paper bag, I walked down the street with no where to go, and no idea what

I was going to do. As I passed an office building that sat right behind Synacore, across the street, I noticed the owner. I'd gotten to know him pretty well from his visits to the facility. He was a real nice man who was very supportive of people trying to turn their lives around.

"Hey, how ya doin'," I greeted him, holding my hand out for a shake.

"Clifford! What are you doing out here by yourself?"

"I left Synacore," I said, going on to explain exactly why I walked out. He listened intently. We had a certain rapport, so I decided to throw a hook out to see what I could reel in.

"I'd sure like a job."

"A job?"

"Yes. You got anything I can do?"

"Well, you can run the elevator in my building, if you want to. It's an easy job, but it doesn't pay much—"

"I'll take it."

And his kindness didn't end there. This man took me to J.C. Penneys, spending over $100 on clothes for me—pants, two shirts, socks, and a pair of shoes.

I rented a room at a nearby YMCA, and went to work the very next day. Synacore employees couldn't help but see me going in and out of the office building everyday, and I got a charge out of that. It might have been stupid of me to stay in the immediate vicinity, but I couldn't help it. I enjoyed flaunting my freedom in their faces.

Freedom lasted a little more than two weeks. In my room one evening, I heard a knock at the door. I opened it to see two policemen standing there.

"Clifford Harris?"

"Yes?"

"You're under arrest." The police whirled me around, hand-

148

cuffing my wrists together in one smooth motion.

"Aw come on man, what you doing? What's going on?" They told me I had violated my prison term by leaving Synacore, and Synacore wanted me out of the area.

I spent two weeks in custody in Long Beach, before they flew me back to Denver. As a convicted criminal, I was required to remain handcuffed through the entire trip. A Black man—walking through the airport in handcuffs—"Must be a fugitive, hunted down for murder, or some other heinous crime", at least that's what the staring faces of the people seemed to say, passing their judgments on me as I walked through the terminal and sat on the plane.

Back in Denver, I stood before the judge, awaiting my fate, ready to go back to jail. Scanning my file, a puzzled look crossed the judge's face.

"Why is this man here?"

The prosecutor launched into his story but the judge interrupted him.

"He hasn't committed a crime."

The prosecutor picked up where he'd been interrupted, forcefully stating his case. I can't even remember the conversation, but he and the judge talked back and forth, until the judge said—

"Case closed. You're free to go Mr. Harris."

WHAT? Did I hear that right? I was free to go? Oh my goodness! I was flabbergasted. I couldn't believe it. I was home, and free to go! Talk about a man wanting to dance down the aisle, I felt just like doing that. I was ready for a huge celebration.

And celebrate I did. I pranced out of jail into the Denver night air, right on down to the nearest drug dealer, and bought me some heroin. I had lost absolutely nothing during my

Synacore stint—nothing but time.

Years later, Synacore closed down, the program and the owners totally discredited. But I was already proof that a man with a demon couldn't be stopped. By anything.

The path of the righteous is like the first gleam of dawn, shining ever brighter till the full light of day. But the way of the wicked is like deep darkness; they do not know what makes them stumble.
Proverbs 4:18,19

Chapter 11

GAGE

As you live life, you expect certain people to stick by you through the good as well as the bad—your spouse, children, parents, brothers and sisters. It's very rare when you're blessed with a friend who believes in you, no matter what condition you find yourself in. It's even more rare when that friend is of a different race.

I first met Gage Behunin in 1964. A White man of medium height and stocky build, with a receding hairline. Gage was about five years older than me. He had strongly religious ties, like me—he and his family were devout Mormons—but unlike me, he still practiced his beliefs.

Gage was a bricklayer who eventually became a big-time developer with his own construction company. We met after his foreman hired daddy and me as bricklayers to help build dormitories at the state university in Boulder, Colorado. Being young, I showed off. I prided myself in doing quality work, but fast. Regularly, I finished laying my line of brick before anyone else. While waiting for everyone to catch up, I took my down time to stretch and relax.

On one of those days, as usual, I stood around on the job site, stretching out my body and watching the other guys lay brick. I noticed Gage standing a few feet from me, staring. His presence didn't faze me—he being the boss and all—because I had finished my work, for the time being. After a little while, Gage sauntered over to me.

"Why are you just standing around?" His blue eyes looked into my brown ones questioningly. "Why aren't you helping to get this done?"

Never answering his question, I bent down and proceeded to help the man next to me. Gage turned around and walked away.

On Friday, daddy and I went to pick up our paychecks. Opening his envelope, I heard daddy suck in his breath. His brow furrowed into tiny lines, as he struggled to keep his composure.

"What's the matter," I asked him.

"They fired me." His voice registered disbelief as his mind searched for a reason why.

"WHAT! You gotta be kidding."

"No, I'm not. They fired me. I've got two checks here—one for my week's work and one for severance pay."

I was in as much shock as daddy. He was the kind of employee one always wants on the job; dedicated and hardworking, with high quality skills. His work was always better than anybody else's. We'd only been on the job for about three or four weeks.

Confused and humiliated, daddy muttered to himself all the way to the car. I stopped asking him questions and expressing my amazement at this weird turn of events. I didn't want to impose on his pain. The least I could do was allow him to walk away with some dignity. Besides, I knew daddy would get another job almost immediately.

Monday morning I went to work. Sometime in the middle of the morning, Gage came to the job site. Seeing me working, he ran toward me, yelling.

"HEY, WHAT ARE YOU DOING HERE?" His face clouded over with anger.

"What do you mean what am I doing here? I'm working."

Looking around, eyes searching, Gage asked "where's your dad?"

What kind of question is that, I wondered to myself. He knows good and well where my dad is, but I obliged him with an answer anyway.

"You FIRED him," I shot back, somewhat accusingly.

Gage looked at me with surprise. "NO I DIDN'T. I FIRED YOU!" He threw a finger and his head in my direction.

"ME?" Gage's words were like ice cold water thrown in my face.

"YES, YOU." Gage's emphatically punctuated his reply with a hard nod of his head. "Every time I come on the job site, YOU'RE the one always standing around doing nothing, watching everybody else work. NOT your daddy."

Upset at the apparent mix-up of his instructions, Gage waved me away telling me to go home and ask my daddy back to the job. Now I knew, first-hand, how daddy felt when he thought he was fired. Just that quickly, I wore the shoe on my foot.

Daddy's reaction to the news was conflicted. He was elated that the firing wasn't his firing after all. But he felt bad that it was meant for me. This time, I muttered in disbelief.

"I can't believe they fired me," I said to daddy. "You know I'm a good worker, and a GOOD bricklayer—you taught me everything I know."

"I know son..." I heard the bitter sweetness in daddy's voice. He promised to try and get me back on the job.

The next morning, I went to the job site with daddy and waited for Gage to show up. I rehearsed over and over in my mind what I wanted to say to him, swallowing down the mild anxiety and nervousness keeping me edgy. When Gage saw me, he unhesitatingly walked right over to me, incredulous to see my face yet another time. Before a sound could escape his mouth, I started my well-rehearsed speech.

"Look," I said, "I know every time you've come to the job you've seen me just standing around and I'm really sorry about that."

Gage listened intently while I begged him to take me back. I promised to work hard, not only doing my work, but helping everybody else too. I told him I'd just gotten married and I really needed the job. I told him he wouldn't be sorry if he hired me back.

When my steam ran out, we stood staring into each other's face, the sounds of work filling the gap between us.

"Okay." Gage responded. I didn't realize I'd been holding my breath until that moment. "I'll take you back, but I expect a full day's work from you."

"Oh, you'll get that," I grinned hard, "I promise, Chief."

And I kept my word. I worked harder than any other employee around that job site. Everybody knew it, 'cause everybody saw it. Eventually, Chief got the word and was pleased I hadn't disappointed him.

Gage and I took a strong, silent liking to each other. I got to know his wife and children very well—so well that Gage invited me to his daughter's wedding. And there I was, this one little Black man in a sea of White, Mormon faces.

Though no one else could see it, we knew something unexplainable bonded us together. It was unexplainable, because the bond remained no matter how hard I tried to sever it.

It was Gage who loaned me the $800 for the down payment on my house. When I had no transportation, it was Gage who sold me his daughter's 1965 Mustang, on credit, when she'd gotten a new car. He even paid the insurance for me. And when I needed money to finance my growing drug habit, it was Gage I stole from.

Early one morning before work, I went to Gage's shop, located out in the Denver suburbs. Surprisingly, though not one soul was around, the shop door was open. Walking inside, I stopped and looked around. My eyes fell on two semi-tractor trailer tires and a bell went off in my head. I had stopped stealing from my own house to support my growing drug habit and was looking for other ways to get cash. The two tires flashed neon lights at me, screaming "SELL ME. SELL ME."

Excitedly, I walked over to the tires and ran my fingers lightly over the hard, grooved rubber. I inhaled the new rubber smell. One by one I rolled the tires out to my car, not even thinking about how I was going to fit these huge tires into my tiny Mustang. Undaunted, I pushed and shoved, forcing the tires into the trunk. They went in only far enough to not fall out. With a good portion the tires sticking out of the car, I drove off for Denver, patting myself on the back for my good fortune.

About ten blocks from my destination, the flashing blue light of a police car appeared in my rearview mirror, just over the top of the open trunk. I pulled the car over on the road side.

"What's the problem officer?" I spoke as if seeing a Black man driving a tiny Mustang through the Denver ghetto, with two semi-tractor trailer tires poking out of the trunk, was an everyday occurrence.

"Where are you going with those tires?"

"I'm going home, officer."

"Where'd you get 'em?"

"I got 'em from my job. My boss let me have 'em," I replied calmly.

"What for? They don't fit your car."

"Well, I'm not going to use them for my car..."

"So what are going to do with them?"

I couldn't explain what I was going to do with them, because I planned to sell them. Why then, the policeman wanted to know, would my boss give me the tires?

I smiled and shrugged my shoulders. "I don't know," I replied, looking up into his face.

"Mm-hm. Why don't we take a little trip on down to the police station and we'll call your boss and check it out."

Even though I was busted, I played the game through. I listened as the policeman relayed the story over the phone with a smirky voice. I heard him ask "did you give him permission to take the tires?"

The smirk disappeared from his voice and his face as Gage's answer burned his ears. His body lost some of its power posture, his self-important confidence watered down. Hanging up the phone, he looked at me with resignation, grudgingly telling me I was free to go because Gage had backed up my lie.

I leaped in the air, inside my head, keeping my exterior calm. I stood a little taller and thanked the policeman with a that's-what-you-get-for-thinking-I-was-lying attitude.

I walked away thanking Gage for keeping my butt out of jail. *One day I'll repay him*, I thought, *but right now, I've got to go sell those tires*. The drugs were calling my name and they were my only priority.

I went to work the next morning, uninhibited by my actions of the previous day. After all, I was a responsible employee who took my job seriously, especially since my opportunities to work were sporadic. When Gage saw me, our eyes locked, transmitting all the words too trite to say verbally. I choked with guilt, waiting to be crushed by the weight of Gage's

156

wrath, like a worm under foot. Instead, he said nothing. He went about his work and I went about mine.

My self-loathing lasted until I succumbed to my next boiling urge for drugs. We were completing a job building new units in office complexes and Gage had received a shipment of brand new furnaces for the units. Each furnace cost between $1,500 and $2,000. Badly in need of money, I thought maybe I could interest someone in purchasing them from me. I contacted a potential buyer.

"Hey Sipio," I greeted my friend.

"Whatsup Clifford."

"I got something you might be interested in..." I launched into the story about the new furnaces, while Sipio listened intently. Sipio and I had known each other for years. He owned a gas station that did a fair business, and he made money on the side selling stolen stuff he bought from me, like tires. Sipio's gas station also served as a hang out for many of the Black men in the area. Often, we used his gas station as a shooting gallery.

"So whataya say, man?" I asked as I finished my proposition.

"What the h— am I gonna do with some d— furnaces?

"S— man, I don't care what you do with 'em. I KNOW you can find a way to make somethin' off 'em."

"What you selling 'em for?" Having no sense of real value, I just came up with a figure that sounded like enough money to do what I needed to do.

"Uh, a hundred dollars a piece." Sipio thought for a minute.

"Oh, alright."

Elated, I laid my plans for stealing the furnaces. Since it was summertime, it would still be daylight after the construction site closed down for the evening. I picked my time and waited.

On the evening I picked to burglarize my job site, I left at knock-off time, but returned late enough when I knew everyone was gone. Climbing into the cab of a forklift, I drove the machine to the merchandise. Tenderly, I guided the machine's prongs under the furnace—still packed in its box—gently lifting each one and depositing it on the back of the company truck.

After loading all ten furnaces, I drove to Sipio's, dropped them off, got my money, and returned the truck to the construction site.

When I got to work the next morning, I saw Gage standing at the spot where his $20,000 worth of brand, new furnaces once stood. I walked over to him. With his hands on his hips, head bowed and face fire engine red, he barely noticed me.

"Mornin' Chief," I said with a voice probably a little to chipper. Gage could hardly croak out a response, using most of his energy to control his anger. "What's wrong?" I asked.

"Somebody ripped me off, that's what's wrong. All my furnaces gone. $20,000 friggin' dollars down the drain." Gage fought hard to keep his emotions in check. My mind screamed "not just somebody, your friend—the man standing right next to you. Open your eyes...put two and two together.

I never told Gage I was the thief. Instead, I let him think what he wanted, though I beat myself down with remorse for repaying all of his kindness and trust by stealing from him. But I couldn't help it. The grip of drugs on my life was too strong to fight. Whenever they called, I answered.

Gage eventually realized I had a drug problem, because there were several times I literally begged him for money, when I wasn't stealing from him. Many times I went to his house late at night to ask for a loan.

"Please, Gage. I need some money," I pleaded with him.

"I don't have any money, Clifford," he countered. But a drug addict doesn't know the meaning of the word "No." Actually, there is no such word. I refused to leave his house until I walked away with some cash. I literally cried, imploring him just to give me a loan, which he eventually did, probably just to get rid of me.

"Here Clifford," he said, handing me $50 or $100 . Thanking him profusely, I promptly went out and bought my next fix.

Regardless of how many times this scene played, Gage always treated me a little better on the job, than all the other workers. If we were building apartments and staying on the premises, he gave me the biggest apartment to stay in alone, while everyone else share apartments.

Gage wasn't the only person I stole from. I conned just about every man who worked for him. Being the only Black employee out of 40 men, I supported every stereotype they probably thought about us.

I came up with some of the best investment deals you can imagine to get my co-workers to give me money. They fell for anything that sounded legitimate that promised to double whatever they gave me. Even the foreman and superintendent fell for the stories. I got $200 from one, $400 from another and $100 from someone else.

Of course I used the money to finance my drug habit. Sooner or later the guys came calling for pay back.

"Clifford, I need my money. When you payin' me back?" was a common phrase spoken like a record stuck on a scratch. Each time, I put the inquiry off by giving some lame excuse of how I was working on it, or just as soon as I got paid, or what-ever sounded plausible.

It took me owing the fellas almost $1,000 before they got fed up with my excuses and went to Gage.

"Gage, you gotta do something about Harris."

"Yeah, you need to fire his a—."

Gage listened to the familiar story as the guys told him about my con games. No one said I shirked on the job or did shoddy work. I was just personally a menace to have around. Unsafe. Criminal.

"How much does he owe you?"

Gage counted out each man's amount, once again bailing me out by paying my debt. But he didn't leave it at that. Calling me to his office, Gage confronted me.

"Clifford..." Gage heaved an exasperated sigh. "What is wrong with you? You're always conning people outta money, never paying anybody back. Why do you keep doing this crap?"

"I don't know Chief, I don't know."

"Well it's gotten outta hand and it's got to stop..."

"You're right, Chief. I've been wrong..."

"And I'm not gonna keep bailing you out. In fact, *you will* pay back the money I gave them to settle your debts."

"I understand, Chief. No problem. And I'm gonna stop. I promise. I won't do nothing like that again." And Gage made sure I paid him back, by deducting a little money out of my check each payday.

Though Gage tolerated my games and drug use, he wasn't a push over. He had his limits too, like the time I asked for a raise and he said no. Flat out, no.

"But don't you think I deserve one?" I asked him.

"Yes."

"So can I have one?"

"No."

And that was it. No explanation. No discussion. Just, no. And I accepted that without any attitude, because if anybody had my back all the time, it was Gage. Several times, during my jail stints, he sent me a little cash. When I was released, he always gave me a job when I called. His consistent kindness didn't just stop with me. He extended it to members of my family as well.

Gage's other employees were very aware of our special relationship, and it spawned plenty of jealousy. Sitting at my table, years later, Gage told me how many of his employees encouraged him, more than once, to fire me. But he just let them know, "I'm the one who makes the decisions to let people go or stay, and Clifford stays."

Oh that everyone could experience a friend like Gage. No matter how hard I tested our friendship or tried to pull it apart, he never budged. I truly took him for granted during the years I wrestled with my demons.

*...there is a friend
who sticks closer than a brother.
Proverbs 18:24*

Chapter 12

GOING BACK

L ife, as I lived it, had no real purpose, no real meaning. My nomadic existence—in and out of jail, working on and off, roaming here and there—provided no stability, no rhyme or reason. Thoughts of my family, Evelyn and the kids, crept into my waking moments, soon occupying a lot more time than I admitted.

I missed my family, especially Stephen, Jeffrey and Rhonda. We hadn't kept in touch since I'd left. They were all in their teen years now, doing all the things teenagers do, and I wasn't part of their lives. I desperately wanted to be.

I'm not sure what prompted my desire to reunite with my family. Values are hard to shake when they've been rooted since childhood, especially with solid examples like daddy and mama. Regardless of the mess I'd made of my life so far, I still wanted to be the husband and father my daddy was. I wanted to put my family back together. If I did that, I believed my life would straighten out.

How to do it, was the question. Do I just show up on the doorstep one day, and say "Hi, I want to come back home?" Hardly. Evelyn probably wouldn't let me step onto the driveway, let alone on the doorstep. The best thing to do, I decided, was to call. Nervous anticipation of Evelyn's reaction made my fingers flutter as I dialed her number.

"Hello?" Evelyn's voice brought back a flood of memories.

"Hi, Evelyn. This is Clifford." An awkward silence ensued. I struggled to fill it. "How's everything going?"

"Fine."

"That's great."

"What do you want?" Evelyn's cold, steel voice left no doubt she really didn't want to talk to me.

"Nothing, nothing. I just called to see how you and the kids are doing."

"Mm hm. Well, we're all doing great, Clifford. Real good."

"So, what you been up to?"

"Clifford, I gotta go."

"Wait—I just wanna talk—"

"About what? We ain't got nothin' to talk about Clifford. I'm real busy. I've got to go, now."

"Well, I'll call you later." I was insistent about reestablishing contact with her.

"No need." She was insistent about keeping me away.

I sighed heavily as I nestled the phone receiver back into its cradle. Reuniting with Evelyn looked like mission impossible. She wanted nothing to do with me, and I couldn't blame her. My track record as a husband and father was at a deficit. They got nothing from me but heartache and pain.

To win her back, I thought, *I'll just do the opposite.* Evelyn had plenty reasons to not want me. I needed to give her just as many reasons to want me. Gritting my teeth with determination, I readied myself for battle. Whatever I had to do to get my family back together, I committed myself to doing.

A couple of days went by before I called Evelyn again.

"What do you want, Clifford?" That familiar tone hadn't changed.

"Nothing. I'm just calling to say hi."

"Clifford—I told you before, you don't need to call here. The kids are fine. I'm fine."

"I know, I just want—"

"Bye, Clifford."

"WAIT EVELYN, PLEASE. Don't hang up. Just let me say this..." I paused a second to see if I was talking to a dial tone. No, she was still on the phone.

"I want to apologize for how I treated you and the children. I perfectly understand you not wanting to talk to me. You have every right in the world to hate me. I did some really horrible things, and while I can't change them, I can say I'm sorry. I hope you can find it in your heart, some day, to forgive me. That's all."

As the sound faded from the phone, I let the dark silence settle between us. Eventually, Evelyn broke the barrier.

"Thanks for apologizing, Clifford." The edges of her voice softened a little. It was minute, but I could tell. "I've got to go now. Take care."

I didn't push the conversation. What I said needed time to sink into her soul. No need to rush things. Patience would win this battle.

I called Evelyn every few days like clockwork. I didn't call too often—just regular enough to show her I was serious about staying in contact. Little by little, I chipped away her resistance to talking with me. I let her know what was happening in my life, and how much I'd changed.

"Really, I'm serious. I'm clean Evelyn. I haven't been on drugs for a good while."

"Yeah RIGHT, Clifford. And when you were living here, you weren't on drugs at all, remember?" She had a point.

"I know you don't believe me, and why should you? I haven't given you any reason to trust me. But I will." And I meant that. I really had been heroin free for about eight months, though I still smoked weed. But that didn't count. Weed wasn't hard drugs.

Evelyn needed proof I had changed, not just words. She had to see with her own eyes that I was a different man from the one who'd moved out years before. I called up Gage and asked for work. He sent me to a job in Wyoming. I called Evelyn before I left, to let her know. I promised to stay in contact. What I didn't say was how I'd planned to send her money. No more words, just action.

I went to work with Gage in Rock Springs, Wyoming, a small city with a predominately White population. The first paycheck I got, I took money out for Evelyn and mailed it to her. It felt pretty exhilarating. Even during my roughest periods of heroin use, I still wanted to take care of my children. I never stopped wanting to be a decent father. A good father. A responsible father. I was finally fulfilling this desire.

"Hey Evelyn," I grinned into the phone during one of my regular calls. "Did you get the money?"

"Yes, Clifford. But what is it for?"

I launched into my appreciation for all she did and how I was sorry I hadn't been able to help her financially with the children. But now I was seizing the chance to contribute, determined to take full advantage of it by doing what I should have been doing all along...

And I did. Each week, I sent money to Evelyn in a sincere effort to prove I was a changed man. After several weeks, and several increasingly pleasant phone conversations, I decided to take a major leap in my reunification plan.

"Evelyn," I told her one night, "I'm coming to Denver for the weekend and I'd like to see you. Maybe we could go out to dinner, or something?" I held my breath, waiting to either be shot to pieces or encouraged. She did neither.

"Sure, why not. I'd like that."

WHAT? She actually accepted a date with me? Stunned, I fought to keep myself from stammering a response so I could maintain my confident demeanor. What progress. We'd actually gone from Evelyn not even entertaining the thought of a conversation with me, to going on a date. I couldn't wait to get home.

Standing on the doorstep of Harris mansion, I pinched myself to make sure it was real. A couple of months ago, I couldn't imagine Evelyn allowing me onto the driveway. Now, Evelyn was inviting me into the house.

I wasn't sure what to do when I saw her. Shake her hand, reach out for a hug, kiss her on the cheek. I felt fourteen again, giddy and unsure of myself. I decided to do nothing and just follow her lead.

"You're looking well, Clifford," Evelyn said, gesturing to me to sit down.

"I feel good," I acknowledged, "but you're the one looking great." Evelyn did look good, less stressed. Oh, she was still working very hard to support our family, but without my mess, she had peace, and it showed.

"Hi dad." A small, timid voice punctured the air and I turned my head to see Stephen, Jeffrey and Rhonda standing there. Tears welled in my eyes as I realized how long it had been since I'd seen them. These weren't the same little kids I'd left years ago. These were young, blossoming adults. Seeing how much they changed pounded home how much I'd missed. It also reinforced my determination not to miss anymore of their lives.

That weekend started a new beginning for the Clifford Harris family. After a couple of months of dating, I asked Evelyn to remarry me. Still apprehensive, she refused. But I didn't let up. I had worn her resistance down to this point, I could certainly be patient enough for her to eventually say "yes."

————•————

Though still heroin free, I battled the urge everyday to renege and give in to my body's urgings. Smoking weed slightly dulled the itch. But trying to keep a stash was getting expensive, especially now that I sent money to Evelyn each week.

To supplement the income I received working construction, I took on a second job dealing drugs for George. Our arrangement allowed me to have a good supply of free weed to smoke, and a supply to sell for extra pocket cash.

Every Tuesday, George shipped two pounds of weed from Denver to Wyoming by Greyhound Bus, which I picked up around 7:30 p.m. I took out enough weed for myself, then sold the rest. Other times, on his way back from a drug run to California, George stopped through Rock Springs, dropped off a supply of weed and speed for me to sell, then went on to Denver.

This went on for some time—long enough for the police in Rock Springs to surmise that I was corrupting their little city—and they set out to do something about it.

One Tuesday night I went to the bus station, as usual, to get my package. When the bus pulled in and unloaded, I walked up to the driver.

"Hey, how ya doin'? Got a package for Cliff Harris?" Looking through the varied parcels, the man shook his head.

"Nope, sure don't."

"Are you sure."

"Yeah, I'm sure. You can check for yourself if you want to, but I got nothing for Harris."

Thanking the man, I left the station. Walking to my car, out of the corner of my eye I spotted some men sitting in a car, watching me. I kept my eyes on them as I got in my car. Driving home, I noticed the car following me. Remaining calm, I parked my car in the front of the apartment building where I worked, and lived. I knew the police couldn't arrest me for dealing because they hadn't seen me do anything.

I went to my second-floor apartment, which had windows facing the back of the building, not the street. Nervously I fidgeted, wondering what scheme the police were devising—if anything at all—to get into my place. I had about a half a pound of weed stashed in my apartment. If the police found a way to search my place, I was a goner.

I peeked out the hallway window. About four or five police cars surrounded the front of the building, the men just sort of standing around watching and waiting. Scared of what I thought was an imminent search, I racked my brain trying to come up with a way to get the weed off the premises.

Paranoid, I paced my apartment floor, knowing the police could create a reason to search my room. If they did, Rock Springs would put this Black man under the jail, and I'd never get out. My mind raced trying to figure out a way to get rid of the weed.

Coming up with no elaborate plan, I had no choice but to just walk out of the building. Gathering up the weed, I put it in my pocket. With all the unconcern I could muster, I walked out of the front door of the building, in full view of the detectives and police standing across the street.

As I walked to my car, I expected them to grab me at any moment. My muscles tensed as I struggled to remain nonchalant, never acknowledging their presence. Miraculously, I got to my car without incident, backed it up and drove right past the small crowd gathered in front of my building. Though they intently watched me drive off, they never stopped me.

To this day, I have no idea why the police never bothered me. Maybe they knew I didn't pick up a package that night and were just sending me a signal that they had an idea I was up to no good. Whatever the reason, that still, small voice popped up again, imploring me to stop what I was doing. I am struck with the irony of God giving me yet another chance to get out of the dangerous game I was playing.

Once I returned home, I called George in Denver.

"Hey man, I never got the package," I informed him. "But you gotta stop sending me stuff, now, 'cause the cops are on to me."

That phone call officially ended my drug dealing days. Always having to watch my back became too stressful. Colorado's drug laws were tough on users, and even tougher on dealers. That close call scared me—not enough to stop doing drugs—just to stop selling them. From then on I only sold drugs as the ultimate last resort for getting a fix.

— — — — • — — — —

Each weekend I went to Denver I asked Evelyn to remarry me. Each weekend she said "no," but I wasn't discouraged. She kept a flicker of hope alive by not turning me away. So I just kept asking, believing all the while the "yes" was coming. Meanwhile, I concentrated on rebuilding my relationship with the children. A couple of times I took them back to Rock Springs with me to visit a few days.

On one of their visits, Bessie came around to hang out.

"I'd like you to meet my children," I offered. "This is Bessie, a friend of mine."

Actually, Bessie was my girlfriend, but I couldn't tell them that. I was trying to get back with their mother. I carefully treated Bessie with a casualness depicting us as nothing more than buddies. I believe the children accepted her as such, until my cover almost blew off.

On one of the children's visit, Bessie and I were in my bedroom lying on the bed, cuddling. I never thought any of the children would open my bedroom door without knocking. But lo and behold, Jeffrey did just that and saw us. I tried to act like what he saw was nothing wrong, but I felt caught. I was ashamed that my son saw me with another woman, particularly when I was trying to reunite with Evelyn.

After that incident, I stepped up my campaign to remarry Evelyn. After much prodding, charming, dating, and proving myself, Evelyn finally agreed. I shared the good news with one of my sisters.

"Clifford," she warned, "that's not a very good idea."

"Why do you say that?"

"Because, nothing's changed. If you remarry her, mark my words, you're going to relapse."

"I will not. I've changed. I know everything was my fault the first time, and this time it will be different. I'm going to show Evelyn that I know how to be the leader in our family."

I really felt I could do it right this time. I knew, if given a second chance, I could prove to everyone I could be the husband and father my daddy taught me to be. I blamed drugs and my friends for all the problems that led to our divorce. I'd be careful this time, to not let that happen again.

For some reason, once Evelyn agreed to marry me, I wouldn't set a date. Several times she asked us to do so, but I kept procrastinating. "We'll do it, baby," I'd reassure her. "There's no rush." But my excuses got old, fast.

"Look Clifford," she finally insisted, "You were so anxious to get married, so let's do it."

I knew I couldn't put if off any longer. We flew to Las Vegas and got married. Hardly hours had passed after saying "I do," before we had a huge argument. I can't even remember what it was about. But we both ended up screaming and yelling at each other, and going to bed mad.

I refused to let that setback hinder me from accomplishing my goal. This remarriage was going to work, or my life was doomed. I couldn't see then, how prophetic my inner pronouncement was.

For what I do
is not the good I want to do;
no, the evil I do not want to do—this
I keep on doing.
Romans 7:19

Chapter 13

BIGTIME

Naw man, I don't want to do that," I told Lennie's brother,
Frank*

"Aw come on man, it's easy. Nobody will see us cause
nobody will be around. They live in the suburbs and the house
is isolated. Nobody is around ALL DAY, so what's the problem?"

I shook my head. Frank was trying to convince me to burglarize a house with him, and I didn't want to do it. I had no
problem stealing from construction sites. They were familiar
territory. But breaking into houses scared me, which is weird
because nothing else seemed to.

"I don't know, man" I kept saying to Frank, shaking my
head. Once again, something—or possibly someone—held me
back.

Frank pushed me hard, enticing me with all the stuff we
could sell and all the money we'd get. He knew a lot about the
house and the quality of its treasures, because his mama
worked there as a maid, part-time.

"Come on, I'm tellin' ya man. That stuff will give us some
serious bank. Nothin' to it. I promise."

"Oh, what the h—," I finally agreed. We jumped into my station wagon and headed for the big house.

"Here, this is it. Turn right here." I steered the car onto a
driveway that wound itself around, far away from the street
and anybody's view. Money screamed from the immaculately

*Name has been changed.

manicured lawn and shrubs, and the huge house that rose up out of the woods like a majestic mountain.

So far, so good. Everything was just as Frank said—isolated, nobody around. I relaxed, just a little. We stopped in the driveway in front of the house. Standing on the porch, dwarfed by the enormity of the house, I asked "How we gonna get in?"

"Like this," and immediately I heard the tinkle of shattering glass as Frank broke a window, climbed inside, and opened the front door.

"Ta da." Frank held the door open for me. Amazingly, the house was not protected by a burglar alarm. Frank already knew this.

I stepped into plush surroundings, trying to feel brave about what I was getting ready to do. I eyed the Victorian furniture. Nice stuff! "Well," I motioned to Frank, "let's get started so we can get outta here."

"Okay," Frank nodded. "You take the upstairs and I'll take downstairs. We'll only take the stuff we can sell fast."

We set to work, quickly filling the car with paintings, T.Vs, antiques, cameras, a vacuum cleaner, and rifles. I couldn't help but start counting in my head the dope this hit would allow me to buy. Soon, the car was stuffed. All these people's possessions were stacked on top of each other in full view through my station wagon's windows.

I stepped outside after one of my trips into the house, an expensive stereo cradled in my arms, when I heard the sound of a car. A Mercedes Benz swung into sight, a middle-aged woman at the wheel. Frank took off running. I stood frozen, staring at her and her car, blocking my way to mine.

I instantly calculated my options. I couldn't drive off because she was in the way. I couldn't run on foot, because the car was registered in my name, so what good would that do? It wasn't like the woman couldn't see all her valuables practically spilling from the sides of my car. I set the stereo down.

Slowly, the woman opened her car door, planting one foot on the ground. All the time keeping her eyes trained on me, she got out. Her face exuded a mixture of puzzles and nerves. With deliberate steps, she walked right up to me.

"What are you doing?"

I pulled myself up a little straighter, trying to intimidate her with my size. With humble matter-of-factness I answered "I'm taking your stuff."

"Would you put it back?"

I matched the woman's gaze, a little taken aback by the simple request. With no real options, I figured why not.

"Yeah."

And that's what I did. I commenced to taking everything out of the car and returning it to the house. She nervously stood by the door, watching me walk in and out, as her possessions paraded in front of her face. After several minutes, she stepped inside and disappeared.

On my last trip into the house, I saw her sitting at a desk writing something. Hearing my footsteps, she gasped and jumped, a look of fear crossing her face like a trapped animal facing certain death.

We both knew she was writing down my license plate number. If I was a violent criminal, I could have hurt or killed her. But that wasn't me. I didn't even take the paper away from her. Without a word, I just laid the last box down on the floor, turned around and walked out of the house, knowing I was busted.

Driving away, my head began to pound as reality sank in. I knew it would be only a matter of hours before the police hunted me down. I had to get out of town. Once home, I ran to the phone and called Gage.

"Please, please be home," I prayed. Gage was in and out of town all the time and this time, I needed him to be home. My heart leaped when the phone picked up.

"Hello?"

"Gage! Hey man this is Clifford."

"Clifford. How you doing?"

"Well actually, I need some work man. Real bad. Out of Denver. You got anything?"

"Yeah, I'm doing a job in Vale I could use some help on."

"Thanks man. Thanks."

After Gage gave me the particulars, I left a note for Evelyn, jumped in the car and headed for Vale, Colorado—home of one of Colorado's beautiful ski resorts that caters to the rich and famous.

I hung around for two weeks, scared to go back to Denver any sooner. When I wasn't working, I browsed the shops and mingled with the tourists. Soon, I got antsy. I had no drug connections in Vale and my body started grumbling. I fought the urges as long as I could before finally deciding to chance it. I would go back to Denver long enough to make a drug connection, then I'd come back.

I returned home on the third weekend, even though I knew I was taking a huge risk. I got my drugs and spent the next two days high. Sunday night, as I walked to my car to drive back to Vale, the police met me in front of my house.

"Clifford Harris?"

"Yes."

"You're under arrest for burglary..." As they read me my rights and handcuffed my wrists, I knew this wasn't going to be just another 90-day sentence.

————•————

"How do you plead?"

"Guilty, your honor."

The judge looked over my file of past offenses, contemplating what my sentence should be. Leaning forward, he spoke directly to me.

"I'm tired of you, Clifford Harris." He lectured me about my behavior and not learning my lesson.

"No more 60 to 90 days, cause you just don't seem to get it. One to five years in the penitentiary." BANG! The gavel slammed on the wooden throne.

One to five years! One to five years! I kept repeating it over and over in my head. I sort of expected that kind of sentence. My burglary was a felony because I'd broken into the woman's house. So I knew I wasn't going to get small time. But that didn't lessen the shock of actually hearing the words "one to five years." It sounded like an eternity.

Sitting in the holding cell, I pondered what one to five meant. The more I turned it over and over, the worse I felt. I lit a cigarette to calm my nerves.

I wouldn't see my kids, for one to five years. I wouldn't have the opportunity to see either of my sisters or their families, for one to five years. I would be confined in a prison, for one to five years.

As the yelling and cursing all around me invaded my thoughts, horrible visions of prison life flooded my mind. Everything I'd ever heard washed me with fear. Gangs. Beatings. RAPES. *That's where you're going, Clifford,* I thought to myself. *No more little county jails. You're joining the big boys—you've graduated to the big time.*

"No way," I muttered out loud to myself. "You ain't gonna survive this kind of sentence. You will have to find a way to get out of this."

"Time to go," the prison guard shouted, opening the bars to the holding cell. Handcuffs clicked around my wrists, and leg shackles held my ankles captive. With tiny baby steps, I shuffled to a van waiting to transport me to Canyon City.

I sat in the van, squashed between two other men. As the van sped down the highway, I wanted to see outside. But I couldn't. The van didn't have windows, just little peep holes. My urge to see outside grew desperate. I needed to soak in the last residues of freedom, before being thrown into confinement.

Straining, I stretched myself up, up, up, to look out the peep holes. I glimpsed the green of the trees and the breadth of the Denver mountains flashing past.

"God help me" I said, to no one in particular—least of all God. Why would he? I had turned my back on him a long, long time ago. Ain't no way God would bother to help me now.

This is it, I kept thinking. *This is the end of my life*. I was truly alone. Not only didn't I have God, but I didn't have mama or daddy, my kids, my sisters or brothers, nor my friends. I thought about Frank, out there free somewhere and me doing time for something I let him convince me to do.

All the guilty feelings I kept at arms length with the drugs, filled me up. Why would anyone be there for you? You've let down every person who's ever trusted you. Maybe you're finally going where you really deserve to be. Prison. Shut away from decent-living people.

I was scared—deathly afraid of the unknown. I had no idea, then, that I was better off than Frank. Years later, Frank's head was blown off with a shotgun, killed by the owner of a store Frank and somebody else were robbing. That somebody else could've been me. Frank convinced me to rob once. Had I gotten away with it, he may have convinced me to do it again.

———•———

The first thing I noticed when they put me in my cell, was the toilet. Paint was peeling off in several different layers, looking like the toilet had been painted over and over and over again. A putrid stench blanketed the toilet corner.

The rest of my cell furniture consisted of a set of bunk beds and a little table. The only company I had in my cell were the rats that scurried around. My stomach churned, and I fiercely determined to do whatever I had to do to get out of that hole.

Some of my fears of prison life evaporated once I got inside. I had no serious trouble with anybody. No fights. No beatings. No rapes. Just claustrophobia.

For the first 90 days, all new prisoners were evaluated. We went to classes and took all kinds of tests. I was in decent health, except for the headaches—which had started while I was waiting to be tried for the burglary charge—and still continued. All during this period, the prison guards kept constant watch over the new inmates. The "get out of jail" scheme I concocted was to make them think I was losing my mind. After about a week, I put my scheme into action.

Every time I was put back in my cell, I put my shoes on top of the little table. Then I just sat on the bunk, looking petrified and fidgety, peering into the corners of the room, staring. Footsteps sounded through the corridor, stopping in front of my cell.

"Hey, what's the matter with you?" the guard asked me.

"Rats," I responded without looking at him. "These rats are in here."

I never moved from the place where I sat on the bunk. Just kept peering and staring at nothing. Each time the guard passed my cell he'd ask if I was okay. Each time I responded the same way.

At mealtimes, the cell doors opened and all the inmates

marched in line to the dining room. While everyone else walked normally, I walked as if scared to put my foot down on the floor. I jerked my head from side to side, looking all around me, taking halting steps, as if scared to step on something.

Once in the dining hall, I picked up my breakfast tray, and with all those 400 or 500 guys in the dining hall, I chose to sit by myself. Placing my tray on the empty table, I just sat. Looking all around, I made no effort to eat the food in front of me. Just eyes darting here and there. A guard ambled over to me.

"What's the problem Harris?" He was unapologetically gruff. I kept my body still, but my eyes darted back and forth.

"Rats. There's rats in here." I made my voice edgy, quietly frantic. "I can't take these rats."

"Whatta you talkin' about Harris? Ain't no rats in here."

"Rats. Every place. All the time. Can't take these rats. I'm afraid of all these rats." The guard screwed up his face in disgust. He walked away. I didn't turn my head or avert my gaze, and made no effort to move.

I performed my ritual—shoes on top of the table, the fidgety, petrified actions, eyes always darting, barely eating my food—over and over, for about a week and a half. No one really became concerned until my health check ups revealed high blood pressure. When the doctor checked me, my blood pressure was something like 200 over 150. Plus, I still suffered with painful headaches. Concerned, he tried to talk to me.

"Your blood pressure's too high. I'm going to give you something to calm you down." He tried to hand me some pills, but I wouldn't take them.

"Come on, take these pills. They'll make you feel better." I shook my head no.

No matter how hard the doctor tried to get me to take the medicine, I refused. After about two weeks, my blood pressure rose to such a dangerous level, they transferred me to the infirmary. There, I enjoyed the perks of being sick—a crank-up bed, a T.V. and a view of the outside. It wasn't out of jail, but at least I was out of my cell.

I played my game so well, they forced me to talk to a psychiatrist. I really acted crazy for him, especially since there was talk about transferring me out of the infirmary. I avoided transfer for about a week before I went back to a cell.

Close to the end of the 90 days, new prisoners were evaluated by prison officials who decided where each should be placed within the penitentiary system. During that time, I discovered the fish hatchery.

The state's fish and game department ran the fish hatchery. State employees who worked for the department lived at this hatchery, with their families, located high up in the mountains. The state allowed low-risk prisoners to work there, living in a camp about ten miles from the actual premises.

Well, this was definitely up my alley. I told the guards I wanted to be placed at the fish camp. When the officials talked to me about it, they voiced their concerns.

"If we send you to camp, will you run?"

"Run from what?" I responded. "Where'm I gonna run to? My record don't show nothing about running. If I run, I'm just gonna git into more trouble than I'm already in. Naw, I ain't running. Just git me away from these rats."

My scheme worked. They assigned me to the state fish hatchery, near Rifle, Colorado, out from the walls of the penitentiary.

— — — — • — — — —

The area where the prisoners lived looked like a primitive

logging camp. We stayed in tiny, rickety trailers, six to eight men in each one. We used the bathroom in outhouses. I remember thinking that when the weather turned cold, my buns were going to freeze up there.

No fence, or anything enclosed the camp. It would have been real easy for me to walk off, but that would've been dumb. The camp was totally isolated, the nearest town far, far away. It wasn't the best scenario, but it was a heck of a lot better than being behind bars.

I worked hard everyday—even Saturdays and Sundays, which wasn't required—cleaning huge fish tanks to prevent allergies and contamination. As usual, I got along with everybody, from the supervisors, to the guards, to the state employees and other prisoners.

One day, a guard called after me. "Hey Harris. You have some visitors."

Puzzled, I followed him, wondering who in the world would be visiting me. As the people came into view, I recognized my baby sister, Sandra, and two of my older sister's daughters.

"Oh my goodness," I laughed ecstatically, grinning until my head hurt. We threw our arms around each other and hugged and hugged.

"How did you guys get up here? How did you know where to find me."

"Evelyn told me where you were," Sandra said. "So we just decided to drive up here and see if we could visit."

I hadn't seen any of my family in so long. For one hour, I forgot about the person I'd become, immersed in reminiscing about the old days. Sandra and the girls brought me up to date on what was happening with old friends, the family, and other people we knew.

They told me about their vacation trip to California, describing all the places they visited. No one mentioned anything about my problems, or asked questions about why I was in prison, or anything. We just focused on good stuff—upbeat stuff, laughing and talking non-stop.

When they finally drove away, my spirit felt rejuvenated. I hadn't felt that good in a really long time. I waved goodbye to them, feeling grateful that someone had taken the risk of reaching out to me.

Other family members knew where I was, but they didn't want to see me. They loved me, but held a lot of resentment for all the crap I'd put them through. And I couldn't blame them.

I so badly wanted to keep that good feeling from my visit, that I went to the chapel with about three or four other guys, and lighted up some weed. We smoked and talked, just shooting the breeze, until we heard footsteps. Snuffing out the cigarettes, we saw the door open. In walked a guard.

"Whatchall doin' in here?" We all shrugged our shoulders, shaking out heads side to side.

"Nothin'. Just talkin'."

"Ya'll ain't just talkin'. I'm sure I smell some marijuana in here. Ya'll smoking marijuana?"

"No, no," we all responded. "We ain't smoking no marijuana."

"Don't give me that s—. I can smell it, plain as day." The guard went on to grill each of us, and I denied smoking anything. I denied it to the hilt, as did the other guys. But for whatever reason, the guard bought my story and expelled the others from the camp, sending them back to the "big house." The penitentiary. That was my first close call.

My second close call came when one of the state employees caught me selling some fish and pocketing the money. The fish hatchery served as a tourist attraction, always busy with visitors coming up to see the whole process. One of the hatchery's prize attractions was the white trout that were cross-bred up there. These were a special breed of fish. Huge fish.

Since I routinely cleaned the fish tanks, I had easy access to the white trout. So I started selling them to the tourists for about $10 a piece. When a hatchery employee caught on to what I was doing, he told me to quit, but he never busted me to anybody else.

Spending time with Sandra and my nieces reawakened my thirst for freedom. I itched for any legal opportunity to be set free. As usual, the answer fell into my lap.

I learned that Colorado state law stipulated that after convicted felons served 120 days of their time, they could go back to court and petition the judge to reconsider their sentence. But, the petition had to be filed before the end of the 120 days. As far as I knew, no one had ever exercised that right. And because no one had ever done it, I wasn't sure if it would work.

Most prisoners thought a judge wouldn't even begin to reconsider the sentence after only 120 days. Other prisoners hated going through the turmoil of being moved from cell to cell, or from one jail to another. So much of the transition is just sitting and waiting, and very restrictive.

Knowing all that, I decided to ask for reconsideration anyway. When I told the other prisoners what I planned to do, they just laughed at me.

"Oh please, Harris. Why you doing that? You know that man ain't gonna change his mind."

That's okay, I thought. *It's worth a try.* Even though I'd be fighting against two cases—the burglary, and a 90-day sentence for violating probation, I filed two petitions to have each of the sentences reconsidered. Along with one petition, I sent along letters written by several of the state employees who worked at the hatchery, vouching for my good attitude and hard work.

After some waiting, I finally got my first court date regarding the burglary in Denver county.

"Judge, this is ridiculous," the District Attorney pleaded at my court appearance. "Look at this man's record. This is not a once-in-a-while occurrence. This man is a career criminal and a drug addict. He has preyed on the good people of this county, time and time again."

The DA talked on and on, painting an evil picture of me, making it sound like I had murdered 17 people. I knew I had done a lot of wrong, but I was nothing like the picture he created. The judge listened intently while the DA concluded his statements.

"Mr. Harris, do you have anything you want to say?"

I stood to my feet. "Yes, your honor." I looked at Judge Barnes, a pretty, blonde woman perched on the bench. I sensed she was a compassionate person.

"I've been wrong and I know it. But I'm not the kind of person he wants you to think I am. I come from a good family, and I have a trade. I've never beaten anyone or hurt anyone. I'm not a violent man, and I don't belong in prison."

I went on to talk about my children and the hardships they were going through. I talked about their financial situation, and how much they needed my help just to have food and clothes. I talked about what a good bricklayer I was, and how much I could help them if I was allowed to work.

"I just want a chance to go back and be with my kids, your honor." With that, I sat down and waited.

"I've heard the arguments of the DA and the comments from Mr. Harris..." The judge acknowledged our arguments and made observations about my past history and current status.

"I hereby rule in favor of probation for Mr. Harris."

BANG! There went that gavel again.

Relief flooded my soul. I won the first round. Now, I just had one more to go. If I won that one too, I'd be a free man.

I went back to the county jail for two or three days, waiting for my second court date. This one was in Arapaho county, regarding a different felony charge. It was for this appearance I had sent the letters written by the hatchery workers. When I stood before the judge at my second hearing, he commented on the letters.

"Mr. Harris, I usually get letters from pastors, teachers, mothers, uncles, and friends. But never in all my years on the bench, have I received anything like this before." He held up all the letters from the state employees at the fish hatchery.

"They say that for the two months you've been there, you've been an exemplary worker and they believe that you deserve a chance." Smiling at me, the judge concluded, "I'm going to give you probation."

Struggling to control my elation, I simply said "thank you, your honor."

As I walked into the fresh air, a free man, I was not blind to my good fortune. I knew the magnitude of the mess I'd gotten into, and I knew how lucky I was to have gotten off so easy. It never crossed my mind, then, to acknowledge God's hand in the situation at all. I congratulated Clifford. Then I gave myself a good talking to.

"*Cliff,*" I asked myself, "*what is your problem? What is it that keeps getting you into these messes? You know what it is. It's that heroin.*"

I had to make an important decision. Was I going to keep

using that nasty stuff and stay in this ugly, vicious cycle? Or, was I going to let it go, so I could straighten out my life?

"You've got to let go," I said with conviction. *"Just stop using it."* I talked myself into a strong determination to get my life back in order. Once back home, I made a phone call.

"Hello Gage, it's Clifford. I need a job."

I was finally on the right road.

Whoever believes in the Son
has eternal life, but
whoever rejects the Son will not see life,
for God's wrath remains on him.
John 3:36

Chapter 14

ROCK BOTTOM

I kicked my heroin habit for eight months. I still smoked weed, but somehow I managed to leave the dope alone. I focused my energies into maintaining a job with Gage, and maintaining my marriage, which really wasn't doing that great.

I thought remarrying Evelyn would help me get my life straight. It was a second chance to prove to my parents, my siblings, myself, that I could be the kind of husband, provider and father my daddy taught me to be. But Evelyn didn't need me to provide for her. And the kids didn't trust me as a father. They all just carried on their lives as they were used to doing. If I was a part of it, great. If not, it really didn't matter.

Once again, I wallowed in self-pity and tattered esteem, which always precipitated intense drug use. This time was no exception. I started using heroin again, but I didn't stay in it for long. Something new came along that unraveled my life the way no other drug had. Cocaine entered my world in 1978.

The first time I tried coke, I didn't like it. After shooting it in my veins the same way I did dope, the euphoric rush filled me with abnormal energy. My eyes felt like they were bulging from their sockets. I couldn't sit down. I couldn't sleep. I was in a constant state of needing to do something, even if it was just moving around. It made me emotionally crazy. I was used to the relaxed, mellow feeling that heroin provided. I hated the up feeling cocaine produced.

But in time, I learned to like it. Then I fell in love with it. I couldn't do without it. After one high crashed me to the ground, I craved to get up again—a worse craving than even heroin produced. The problem, coke's exorbitant price tag.

While $50 worth of heroin could get me at least three hours of high, $50 worth of coke lasted about five minutes. Within FIVE minutes, I plummeted from coke's high, feeling lower than I felt before I started, which only fueled a fierce desire to get back up. $50 to $100 a pop for five minutes strained my purse strings, but I didn't care.

It didn't take very long for Evelyn to suspect that I was back on drugs. As old, familiar behavior patterns emerged, she knew the deal.

"You're using again." She approached me with an air of sadness. No questions, just a stated fact.

"Come on Evelyn, don't do that. We've been through all that already. When we got back together, I told you I was clean. Ain't nothing changed."

"Clifford, please." Her voice lacked the accusatory tones I was accustomed to. "You don't have to deny it. I just want you to get help, and I'm willing to back you."

But as usual, I lied with conviction, though it did not change Evelyn's opinion. She knew the deal, and she left it alone. By 1979 I was between jobs more than I worked. Evelyn never nagged me about my joblessness. She just went on with her business of taking care of the family as if I was not in the house at all. I can't blame her. It was probably the best thing for her to do, rather than stress out like the first time.

Unfortunately, though, our relationship was headed down a travel-worn path.

— — — — • — — — —

For years, during the first time we were married, I had

talked about building a family room onto our house. Evelyn got so excited at the prospect, eagerly waiting for me to build this addition. But I procrastinated and procrastinated, and she kept asking me, "Clifford, when are you going to do the family room?"

"I'll get to it, Evelyn. Stop worrying about it. I'm gonna do it." I brushed her off each time she questioned me.

Back in the house this second time, Evelyn still wanted that addition built. But when I procrastinated again, she didn't bother to wait on me.

"Clifford."

"What?"

"Don't worry about the family room."

"What do you mean?"

"You don't have to build it."

I looked at her in surprise, wondering why the sudden change in urgency. "Why not? You don't want it anymore?"

"Oh no, I want it. But I've called a contractor to come look at the house and give me an estimate on what it will cost."

I couldn't believe my ears. Evelyn had called another builder to come to MY house where I—a career builder—breathed, ate, lived? To build a room onto MY house. *I DON'T THINK SO.* I would never be able to live that down if I allowed that to happen. My brain fast forwarded, imagining me and Evelyn in some argument where she'd finally say "I had to hire somebody to build this room because you couldn't do it." There was no way I was letting that happen.

"Ain't nobody comin' up in here to build nothin' on this house," I responded to Evelyn with authority.

"Too late. I've already called him. He'll be here tomorrow." Evelyn's tone was matter-of-fact. A tone I'd heard so many times before. A tone that said, "I've taken control of this situation and that's that."

Well I didn't care who Evelyn had called. I wasn't letting any other builder into my house to do a job I was well qualified to do myself. This was one time Evelyn was not going to muscle in on my manhood.

When the builder showed up the next day, he walked into a ball of confusion.

"Hey," I greeted him, and not with a smile on my face or a pleasant voice. "We don't need you. I'm doing this job myself. So get on back where you came from." Evelyn intercepted my hostile rejection.

"Uh, excuse me, but I'm the one who called you," Evelyn ushered the man inside. "Come on in and let me show you where I'd like to have the room built."

The man stepped into the house. He tried to conduct his business, but I wasn't having it.

"I ain't kiddin'," I proceeded to interrupt the man's walk-through. "You ain't doing nothin' in here. So just get yo a— on outta my house. Go on. We don't need you. I got this covered."

Evelyn and I proceeded to pull that man apart, like two children pulling opposite arms of a doll. I treated that man uglier and uglier, until he just left. Basically, I ran him out of my house, determined not to have my pride trampled on by Evelyn or anybody else.

A few days after the episode, we received a letter from that contractor telling us we needed some help. He said we needed to get our marriage together, and he was right. We did need to get it together, but him stepping onto my territory wasn't gonna help us do that.

I started digging the foundation for the family room, but I didn't have the money to build a walkway, let alone a whole room. Who did I turn to, but my human savior, Gage. I approached him at work one day and asked for his help.

"Gage, Evelyn wants this family room built onto our house, and I don't really have the money to do it. But she's buggin' me about it, and I was wondering if I could get a loan?"

Not only did Gage loan me money, but he supplied materials as well—windows, carpet, bricks—and paid for a whole lot of other perks he never agreed to. Once I had Gage's support, I decided to go all out. Whatever Evelyn wanted, she got. I had a point to prove.

I had the kitchen redone, contracting a cabinetmaker who did work for Gage, to custom make oak cabinets with the finest material he could get. I hired another of Gage's men to lay carpet, not only in the new room, but throughout the whole house. "Just charge it to Gage," was the way I paid for most everything. Especially since some of the cash Gage initially loaned me went to support my cocaine habit instead of the building project.

Not really paying attention to what was happening, Gage was shocked when he received the bills from the men who'd done work for me. He called me into his office.

"Clifford, what is this?" Gage waved a bunch of bills at me, bills that amounted to well over $12,000. I looked at him, a little chagrined by his surprise.

"Well, you told me to go ahead on and do this."

"Oh no, buddy. I never gave you the okay for all of this." He punctuated the last word with a jerk of his hand holding the bills. Exasperated, Gage shook his head.

"It's done now. But don't think you aren't paying me back. Every cent. You got me, Clifford?"

"Oh yes, Chief. I'll pay you back." And pay him back, I did. I worked 60 and 70-hour weeks, including Saturdays and Sundays, with no pay for nearly four months, until my debt was cleared.

Some days I worked real hard on the family room; other days I did cocaine all day. Miraculously, only one part of the project reflected how much my drug use impaired my judgment.

I wanted to put a wooden stove in the new room. But to do that, I needed to build a brick wall behind the stove so the heat wouldn't hurt the other walls of the room. As I started building this wall I decided to get a little stylish and build an arch in it. After shooting up some coke to get myself started, I worked on this arch. But all the measuring and figuring in the world couldn't help me get that arch straight. It was always a little off center.

I tore it down and started again, but I could never get the arch right. To this day, a trained builder would shake his head at the way that wall looks. Even in my drug stupor, I knew I was doing a shoddy job. But I couldn't fix it. And it still stands, as a reminder of the demons controlling my life at that time.

Besides the arch, the rest of the room looked great. Once I completed the project, I glowed with pride. I stood a little taller, held my back a little straighter, stuck my chest out. And Evelyn was tickled pink. She had her family room, with a new kitchen and new carpet besides. I even sensed her approval of me and the job I had done.

Building that room built my self-confidence as well. Beholding my accomplishment, a thought struck me. Maybe I could start my own construction business. Yeah, why not? I'd been in the business since my teens. I knew all the ins and outs of construction work, plus I was a really good bricklayer. But as quickly as the thought came, it left. I knew I was in no condition to own a business. Besides, it was too much responsibility, and I had all the responsibility I could handle at the moment.

Evelyn and I entered an unspoken truce after the success of the family room. I tried to use the relaxed atmosphere to my advantage by bringing up a topic we'd discussed several times before. This time I thought I could possibly get a different answer because she was feeling a little better about me.

"Evelyn."

"Hm."

"What about putting my name back on the house deed?"

"What about it?"

"Don't you think it's time my name went back on it?"

"Clifford, we've discussed this already. Putting your name back on the deed would mess up my taxes. I can barely afford what I pay now."

No matter what I said, I couldn't budge Evelyn's mind. The tax issue was a smoke screen for the real reason she wouldn't even consider the notion. She had no shred of trust in me. Especially now that she suspected my drug use. A mother hen fiercely protecting her baby chicks, Evelyn was not about to put her children and herself in jeopardy. Unfortunately, she couldn't protect the children from everything.

Rhonda had blossomed into a beautiful sixteen-year-old, standing on the brink of womanhood. Small and petite like her mom had been when we first met, Rhonda was a pretty girl with innocent loyalty. She was my girl. A daddy's girl. One day she bounced over to me, flushed with excitement.

"Daddy, I want you to go to the debutante ball with me." Now that she was sixteen, it was time for her to be presented to society the way any proper girl should be. It really was an occasion to mark her transition from girl to woman.

"All the girls and their fathers are going to march down the

195

aisle together, and I want you there."

"Now where else do you think I'd be? Of course, I'm gonna march with you."

Delighted, Rhonda made plans for us to attend rehearsal. This was going to be one of the biggest nights of her life and we had to make sure to do everything just right. On rehearsal night, the room pulsated with nervous anticipation as all the young ladies chattered and bubbled about the impending event. But I didn't need their energy to fuel me. I was well fueled already—brimming at the top with cocaine.

As the girls and their fathers lined up, I stood beside my precious daughter. When it was our turn to walk down the aisle, I couldn't maintain my balance. Overloaded with coke, I wobbled with a drunken gait.

"Daddy, what's wrong with you," Rhonda whispered to me. "Stand up straight."

I tried, but I couldn't. I never noticed the flush of embarrassment that spread over Rhonda's face as her petite frame supported my six-foot frame down the aisle, to the questioning stares from everyone else in the room.

Needless to say, I didn't show up at the debutante ball.

Years later, when I tried to apologize to Rhonda about that dreadful day and all the other times I screwed up, she listened intently, accepting my explanations and apologies. But her ultimate response was chilling.

"Daddy, I don't want to get close to you. Too many times I put myself out there for you, just to get hurt over and over. I'm scared if I let myself get close to you, you'll just hurt me again."

What was there for me to say? Rhonda, Stephen, Jeffrey and Evelyn had lived through a life of disappointment, pain, and distrust—caused by the habits I could not shake.

_____•_____

For a person with no steady income, cocaine was just too expensive. I resorted to using a cheaper form of cocaine—cheaper in purity and price—called crank. Crank had its own assortment of side effects completely different from what I experienced with pure coke.

After taking crank, my mouth felt like someone stuffed it with a wad of cotton—so dry that even swallowing was near painful. Crank also took away my desire to eat, bathe, change clothes, or brush my teeth for weeks at a time. I didn't care how putrid my body odor was, or how my clothes stuck to me like a second skin. I didn't have time to take care of myself. I only had time to do crank.

Even though I let hygiene fall by the wayside, I had to make myself eat. Two days on crank without food in my stomach made me so nauseous I wanted to vomit, but there was nothing inside to come up. This interfered with my ability to get high. So I'd tear a slice of bread into bite-size pieces, slowly rolling each morsel around in my mouth, activating my saliva glands to moisten the bread enough to swallow. After following with a shot of water, I'd repeat the ritual until I'd eaten a whole slice. The food reactivated my body's receptiveness to the drug.

Cheaper drugs still needed money to buy them, and I resorted to my specialties for getting cash—conning and stealing. As usual, I preyed on those closest to me first, my family.

Stephen's greatest dream was to finish college. After high school, we'd worked together, side by side, doing construction. And though he was good, Stephen didn't want to be stuck doing that for the rest of his life. He'd already attended one year of college and he was determined to go back. So all the money he worked hard to get, he saved with the intention of

197

paying his way through school.

I knew Stephen had this money, and I knew how important college was to him. But my drug habit had top billing for me. If I needed cash to get my fix, that's all I cared about.

"Stephen," I approached him one day. "I've got this great investment opportunity that could make me a lot of money."

"Yeah?"

"Yeah. But the trouble is, I don't have a sizable amount of cash. If you go in with me, we could double our investment and make a good return on the profit."

"I don't know, dad. How can you be sure it's going to work."

"Oh, I KNOW it's going to work. It's fool proof."

"How much do you need?"

"About $300. That's all. And I guarantee, you'll get that back, plus a good profit."

I saw the wheels spinning in Stephen's mind as he pondered my offer. He'd worked so hard for his money, diligently saving every penny. He didn't want to chance any interference with his plans to go to college. But I wasn't taking "no" for an answer.

"It's okay, I promise," I insisted.

"Dad, you know I'm saving my money to pay for college."

"I know, I know."

"I've got to have this $300 back as soon as possible."

"I promise, you'll get it back and more."

Still with some reservation, Stephen gave me the $300. It really doesn't bear saying, but I sank that $300 into cocaine, my personal investment opportunity for myself. And Jeffrey and Rhonda weren't exempt either. I "borrowed" large sums of money from both of them with grandiose promises to pay them back.

Don't think, though, I didn't feel terrible about conning my own children. I did. My lies did near irreparable damage to my relationship with each of them. And that drove me to drugs even more. Soon, I had to resort to my old standby for getting money.

I'd grown extremely skillful at stealing tires from gas stations, and this particular Friday evening I went to a site I'd already ripped off twice before.

I spotted the tires chained to a rack sitting in front of the station building. After checking to make sure all the station employees were busy, I rolled the rack to the back side of the building as if this was my assigned task. I whipped out my cutters, snapping the chains securing the tires.

One by one, I loaded the tires into my station wagon, packing the car tight. I forced myself to stay relaxed and calm, as though I was an employee performing my regular duties. When the car was full, I dropped them off to my buyer.

"This is great, man," my buyer said enthusiastically as he surveyed his purchase. "Can you get me more?"

"I'm not sure, man."

"Ah come on. I'll pay you real good."

Though I needed all the cash I could get, the prospect of hunting for another gas station didn't thrill me. "Oh, what the h—," I thought. "I'll just go back to the station where I got these from and load up the rest of the tires." I made the deal with my buyer and headed back to the scene of my crime to steal again.

I pulled around to the back of the station where I'd left the tire rack. When I got out of the car and walked over to the rack, instantly I was staring down the barrel of a pistol. "I ought to blow your d— head off."

I froze but I wasn't afraid. Somehow I sensed this man wasn't going to pull the trigger.

"You got some nerve bringing your a— back here again after stealing from me once already. If it wasn't for that phone call I got from someone in that hotel who saw you the first time, you would've gotten away with it. I ought to kill you."

The station owner held me at gunpoint until the police came. During my hostage moments, the only thing running through my head was, *d—, I'm gonna have to spend the night in jail*. Actually, that meant having to spend the entire weekend locked up because nobody got released on bail until Monday. A weekend in jail meant a weekend without drugs. That really ticked me off.

As many times before, on Monday I appeared before the judge.

"How do you plead?"

"Guilty your honor."

"I sentence you to serve 90 days." BANG! The gavel cracked the desktop.

It surprised me that the sentence was so light. I was more concerned that this conviction was my second felony. A third felony in Colorado could send me to jail for life. I couldn't let that happen.

A few days after my release, a friend of mine from public school, *Jerry Mason, came by for a visit. Jerry stayed away from the drug scene, but he was a stone alcoholic. He liked his brew and his addiction to liquor was as potent as my drug habit.

"Whassup man?" Jerry greeted me warmly.

"Nothin', man. Same 'ol same 'ol."

"I hear ya, man." I got the feeling Jerry didn't come by for just a casual hello.

"Whassup wit' you?" I inquired.

"Well, I was wondering if I could get your help with somethin'?" My inquisitive expression prodded Jerry to continue.

*Name have been changed.

"See, you know I work at this tractor trailer place, and I was thinkin' how easy it'd be to steal some of their tires."

"Oh no." I shook my head. I just got out of jail for that very thing. Was no way I was putting myself right back into the same situation. Not when I was staring at a possible life sentence if we got caught.

"Sorry man, I can't help you."

"Come on Cliff. I can't do it by myself."

"Then get somebody else, cause I can't take the risk of getting caught."

"We ain't gonna get caught. I promise. I got this planned out, man. I mean, I work there, so I know the place. We won't have to break no doors or nothin', man. I'm gonna have a key and everything."

"You don't understand, Jerry. If, by some stretch of the imagination, we do get caught, you'll get probation and I'll get the penitentiary, and I ain't going back to the penitentiary." Jerry kept insisting that we wouldn't get caught, but I wasn't buying it. He finally threw the punchline.

"Clifford man, we talking about four, five thousand dollars we can get for this stuff, and split it. You know you need the money for Evelyn and the kids. You always fussin' 'bout how Evelyn stays on your back about sending money. Think about it. Two thousand dollars."

Well, I wasn't thinking about the bills two thousand dollars could pay for Evelyn and the kids. I was picturing two thousand dollars worth of coke. But even that delectable thought couldn't shake the trepidation I felt at the prospect.

"I don't know, man. I'm gonna have to think about it."

"Okay, okay man. No problem. You think about it and I'll check back with you later."

I thought about Jerry's proposition for three days, pondering over and over in my mind the likelihood of us getting caught. I weighed his assurances he knew what he was doing. I savored the thought of two thousand dollars worth of coke. The coke won out. Somewhat reluctantly, I agreed to burglarize the garage with him.

"So here's the plan," Jerry filled me in. "Someone's gonna leave the garage door unlocked. We'll load up one of the trucks with tires, drive the truck to a warehouse, unload the stuff, then abandon the truck somewhere. Simple." Right. Simple.

We met around 1:00 on a Sunday morning, in the dark of night. That was my first clue. I never liked sneaking around at night. I was a day thief—an "in your face" kind of thief. Sneaking made me uneasy, and this night was no exception.

We weren't in the building ten minutes before a hoard of policemen descended on us like bees on a honeycomb. It happened so lightening fast, we didn't have time to blink. Before I could make sense of anything, I was flat on my stomach, face down in a puddle of muddy water with a foot fastened to the back of my neck and a shotgun pointed at my head. Every time I raised my head to breathe, the policeman shoved my face back into the puddle.

I can't believe this s—, I thought to myself. I just wanted to kick myself in the butt for going against my intuition and letting Jerry talk me into doing this job. Panic gurgled in my throat.

"What were you guys doing in there?" the cop finally broke his silence. Jerry remained calm, but I was shaken up. I began blabbing the whole story. If I had kept my mouth shut, they would have had no case. We hadn't broken into the garage and nothing was taken. But with all I had become, I still wasn't good at lying. Besides, my life was in the toilet now, anyway.

The police yanked us up off the ground and threw us in the back of the car. With muddy liquid rolling down my face, I sat there, facing the prospect of life in prison. After a couple of days in jail, I was itching to get out, but I had no one to post bail for me. Evelyn wouldn't take my call. Gage was tapped out with saving my back. In total desperation, I called a pawn shop owner with whom I'd done a lot of business.

"Yo, whassup," I began the conversation. "I need you to do me a favor."

"Yeah, what's that?"

"I need you to come post bond for me."

"You want me to do what?" In my mind's eye I could see him screwing up his face in disbelief that I would actually call him and ask him to pay for me to get out of jail.

"I'm in jail and I need you to come get me out."

"What you think this is brothaman? I ain't no personal bank."

"Look, you've made a lot of money off of me with all the stuff I've brought you. You could at least pay me back by doing this one favor for me."

The pawn shop owner protested for a few minutes, but finally relented and agreed to post bond for me. After I got out, I hired a lawyer who fought the case going to trial for an entire year by filing continuance after continuance. Whatever reasons he could come up with, he used—he needed more time, he had to be out of town, he wasn't ready to present my case. As long as I kept paying him, he kept finding ways to postpone the trial.

During the year, my drug use escalated off the chart. I stayed high all the time to deaden the accusatory thoughts that shouted at me constantly. My family acted like I was invisible. Because Colorado is a "three strikes you're out" state, I was facing life in prison. As far as I was concerned, I was at the end of the line. I had no idea the very core of my existence was about to snap.

What a wretched man I am!
Who will rescue me
from this body of death?
Romans 7:24

Chapter 15

DARK MIDNIGHT

Mama is dying."

The voice on the other end of the phone barely registered in my brain as I heard those words. My sister, Melba, had called to tell me mama's cancer was spreading and there was nothing else that could be done.

Mama had been sick for three or four years, but I never thought about her dying. Who wants to picture a parent dying; the person who rocked you to sleep, wiped your runny nose, kissed your hurts, laughed at your silliness, and disciplined with righteous indignation. I couldn't imagine Mama dead, yet I was hearing that it was inevitable.

Guilt gnawed at me. As long as my parents had been in Florida, I had never gone to see them. The only time I initiated contact was to con them out of money for drugs. I used them like I used everybody else, never thinking that one day they wouldn't be around anymore.

Instantly, I knew I had to go visit Mama. What if she died while I was in the penitentiary? I'd never forgive myself for not grabbing the opportunity to spend time with her. I couldn't let her leave this earth without telling her, face to face, how much I loved her. Whatever I had to do, I was going to see her—probably for the last time.

Being out on bond I wasn't supposed to leave the state. But I didn't care. I was determined to see Mama and that's all I considered. I thought about Stephen, Jeffrey and Rhonda.

They needed to see their grandmother. I wasn't sure if Evelyn would let me take them, but it was worth an ask.

"I'm going down to see Mama," I told Evelyn after I got off the phone with Melba. "She's not doing real good, and I want to see her." I hesitated a few seconds. "And I want the children to see her too."

Evelyn's face flickered with doubt as my words sunk into her consciousness. Put her children in my care on a cross-country trip? I'm sure the prospect was chilling. Had she known I was out of jail on bond and required to stay within state lines, "okay" would never have crossed her lips. But without a fight, she consented.

"Sure, Cliff. They need to see their grandmother, so that's fine."

We packed our stuff and piled it and the kids into my Pontiac. With no more than $30 in cash and a stolen credit card I got from a drug buddy, we headed to Florida with Evelyn's words "be careful" still ringing in my ears. Her plea had very little to do with safe driving. We both knew that.

Thirty dollars wasn't much money to feed three teenagers and me, but I made do. The kids never complained about not having enough to eat, or being too cramped, or being tired. Even through my drug haze, it felt good to have them with me.

I used the credit card to buy gas, and at one point, I realized after going 40 or 50 miles down the road that I'd left the stolen credit card at the last gas stop. I couldn't believe it. There was no way we'd finish the trip, or be able to drive back home without that card. Yet, I was scared to death to go back and get it. What if the man had figured out it was stolen and had called the cops? They could be waiting on me. I'd be in deeper hot water than I was in already, and my children would be left at the mercy of strangers.

Regardless of the possible outcomes, I turned the car around anyway, and headed back to the station. I had to have that card back. Thankfully, nothing I'd envisioned happened. The man gave me the credit card and I was on my way again.

Trying to make up for lost time, I raced over the Georgia state line, my foot heavy on the pedal. With very little traffic on the road, I tested the speed limit enforcement a little too hard, flying through the little towns. Next thing I knew, flashing lights appeared in my rearview mirror. A police car encouraging me to pull over on the roadside.

Aw crap! I thought to myself. *This was one thing I didn't need right now.* Not only was I edgy about breaking bond, but I had a stolen credit card and a stash of weed hidden under my car seat. I just knew I was going to get busted and end up in jail. Especially when I saw the policeman. A White cop stopping a Black felon drug addict, in the south! This was not a positive scenario.

Willing myself to remain calm, I rolled down my window.

"Evening officer." I oozed humility and willing cooperation.

The officer stared in my face, then leaned his head somewhat into the car where he surveyed my three children sprawled across the back seat, sleeping.

"Going pretty fast for a 25-mile zone, aren't you?"

"Yes sir, I'm sorry sir. I'm trying to get to Jacksonville to see my dying mother. I guess I got a little anxious."

"May I see your driver's license."

"Sure." I accommodatingly pulled out my license and handed it to him. He walked back to his car. I watched through my rearview as he got inside and called in my name and numbers.

This is it. This is it, I thought. Unconsciously I held my breath, waiting for him to come back and escort me to jail. Sure enough, he came back, stared at the kids—who were by now wide awake, but faking sleep—then said, "I'd like you to follow my car, sir. We're going to the police station."

My heart dropped like a ship anchor into the bottom of my stomach. My blood raced as I thought about my kids. *What kind of stupid fool was I, putting them into this kind of situation. I should have just stayed my butt home, or at least left them home. But NO, I just had to go see Mama at whatever cost.* It was a little late for all these thoughts to come pouring into my head. But hindsight is twenty-twenty. It's even sharper when you know you are wrong.

The drive to the police station was one of the most stressful drives of my life. The overwhelming anticipation of punishment haunted me, making it difficult for me to think straight. I was a sheep being led to slaughter.

At the police station, I waited in the car while the cop went inside. To my utter amazement, they never searched me or the car. Just simply handed me a warning and waved me on my way. I'm not sure which was worse—the anticipation of being arrested then, or later—should something else happen.

I didn't sit around to find out. We arrived in Lake Alford, Florida just before daylight. I wrapped my arms around Mama's waning frame. The cancer was taking its toll on her and it was readily noticeable. A stab of pain shot through my heart as the realization hit me that she really was going to die.

Mama and daddy were ecstatic at seeing the children, and vice versa. After all the huggin' and kissin' was through, we settled down to relax and chat and catch my parents up on the kids' lives. There was nothing much for me to tell them. I just enjoyed being in their company.

It wasn't long before my body began announcing its drug deficit. I was increasingly becoming nervous and jittery. I'd already slipped away a few times to smoke a joint, but that wasn't enough. I needed a cocaine fix, and had no idea where, in little Lake Alford, I could cop some stuff.

By the third day, I couldn't stand it anymore. Waiting until everyone had gone to bed, I got in my car and drove 150 miles to Jacksonville, sure I could find somebody in that city to sell me some coke. Once there, I cruised around looking for downtown. Upon finding downtown, I kept my eyes peeled for the night life. It seemed like hours before I saw anybody who looked like they were about action.

"Yo brotha," I said to a man standing on the street. "I'm lookin for some stuff, you know what I'm talkin 'bout? Some coke."

"Watchu got to pay for it?"

"All I got is $25"

The man reached into his pocket and handed me a small plastic bag. I grabbed it and shot out of there, anxious to cook it up and get it into my system. I couldn't even wait until I got back to Lake Alford. I pulled over on the side of a deserted road and proceeded to heat up the "coke".

"Aw s—," I yelled. I pounded the steering wheel, then bolted out of the car. Kicking the tires and slamming my hands against the car, I erupted in anger. "That a— cheated me. I can't believe he cheated me." I slammed the car again, and let out a blood-curdling yell. My body stood on the brink of going over the edge, and I didn't have a way to save it.

I only had $15 left, which wasn't enough to buy some coke, if I could have even found any. The best I could do was get a couple of bottles of wine and combine that with the weed I had. That was a sad alternative. I had geared up for a cocaine fix, and nothing else would appease that craving.

Despondent, I got back in the car and drove to Lake Alford. On the outskirts of the city, I saw a liquor store and pulled in the parking lot. The insatiable craving for cocaine completely dulled my senses. I really had no idea what I was doing. That was clearly evident once I walked into the store.

"What the h—!" A Black guy looked at me in utter disbelief, his eyes wide and mouth hanging open. The other Black guy stared at me as if I'd just walked out of a mental hospital. The female clerk they were talking to stared at me like I was an alien.

"You crazy, man?" one guy implored, pointing to the joint hanging out the side of my mouth like a common cigarette.

"You can't walk around here doing that."

"Where the h— you from, buddy?" the other one asked. "Surely you're not from around here."

"Come on, let's go outside." The two men, who turned out to be plains-clothes detectives, escorted me to my car. Had I been in my right mind, I would have known instantly what they were.

"You got anymore in your car? If so, you'd better tell us now, cause you going to jail."

"Naw, naw," I shook my head fervently, playing the game to the hilt. "I ain't got no more weed. Uh uh."

The detectives leaned in and searched my car, easily discovering the two or three joints I had hidden under the floor mat.

"Let's go," they said, pulling my arm and motioning to their car. My evening ended with the clang of the cell door as it swung shut. On a visit to Lake Alford, to see my dying mother, with my three children in tow, I ended up in the county jail. Now, I had to call my aging father to come get me, shattering the peace and serenity they enjoyed in this small town. My fingers trembled as I dialed my parents' home.

"Hello, daddy?" Flashbacks seared my brain. Daddy getting the money back I lost gambling. Daddy getting me out of the jail after my first theft. Daddy sending me money for bills that never got paid.

"Daddy. I need you to come get me."

"What do you mean? Where are you?"

I could barely get the words out. I was so ashamed. A grown man begging for my father's help out of a situation I created. Dragging my father into turmoil he didn't need in the twilight years of his life. Infringing on the stress already brewing over Mama's failing health.

"I'm… I'm in the county jail." Daddy heaved a weary sigh. A sigh that bespoke years of frustration, wondering where he went wrong, why I turned out the way I did.

"I'll come get you in the morning."

"Oh no daddy, you got to come tonight."

"Clifford…"

"Uh uh. I can't stay here daddy. My children cannot wake up in the morning and I not be there. That can't happen. You got to get me tonight." I was emphatic. There was no way I could let my children wake up in a home they were visiting, to discover their daddy was in jail. I couldn't let that happen. Thankfully, daddy understood.

"Alright, Clifford. I'll be there soon."

I hated that daddy had to get out of bed in the middle of the night, put on clothes and come out, just to retrieve me. But the little shred of pride I clung to as the father of my children had to be fiercely protected. Evelyn had entrusted them to MY care. We were thousands of miles from home. They needed to think they could depend on me in some minute way.

Daddy paid my bail and they released me. An uneasy silence hung between us. I tried to apologize, but it sounded so hollow. So empty. So fake. Daddy didn't respond. Why should he? I was still acting a fool, after all these years. He couldn't trust me. Nobody could. Nobody wanted to.

As we walked into the house, Mama's gaze met mine. She looked tired. Worn down. Defeated. I couldn't say anything.

"Clifford," she began, with a resigned tone. "You know... I really didn't want you to come down here and see me, cause I knew you were still on that stuff."

Her words were ice cold water thrown in my face. Without saying anything else, she turned and walked away, leaving me in the chill of the air. What was killing her more? The cancer? Or my bringing my mess back into their lives? My mother was dying, and she preferred that her child not be there.

Mama called my brother, Gene, and asked him to come down. Years later, I found out she wanted me out of the house, but was scared I wouldn't leave on my own. Gene was to talk me into leaving. But he never said one word to me that revealed he knew what had happened. I thought he just came to Florida to see me because I was there.

When my case went to court the judge at my trial fined me $300 and told me to leave Florida and never come back again. He didn't have to tell me twice. I was more than ready to go. Daddy paid the fine, gave me a lecture, gave me gas money, and sent us on our way.

The whole trip was a nightmare I desperately wanted to awaken from. Though I could drive away from the scene and never look back, I couldn't drive away from the accusatory voices burning my brain. They scalded me with guilt of what I had done to my parents.

Sadly, this encounter was what I left with Mama. It was the memory of that ruined Clifford she took to her grave. Because I never saw her alive, again.

— — — — • — — — —

Back in Denver, my life plummeted in a downward spiral. I

knew it was just a matter of time before I would be sent back to the penitentiary, so I tried to blow myself apart doing as much coke as I could do everyday. I stole anything I could get my hands on, not caring if I got caught or not. Miraculously, I never did.

My lawyer was still stalling my trial for the attempted burglary with Jerry, even though I got lax with his payments. Eventually, I stopped paying him altogether. I didn't have any money. It was all going to support my drug habit. Several times he threatened to quit, but I always conned him with promises of payment, that he allowed himself to believe. And he'd end up staying.

But my luck ran out, even with that. He did have a breaking point. And when he reached it, he quit. As usual, I was on my own with no one to blame but myself.

When I wasn't stealing, I worked for Gage. I was in Rock Springs, Wyoming when I got a call from Evelyn asking me to come by the house when I got back to Denver. I was going back, to catch a flight to Florida. Mama had gotten worse, and I was going down to see her one last time.

I waited in the house for Evelyn to get off work. She had told me not to go anywhere until she got there. When she walked into the house, I should have sensed something was wrong, but I was not thinking.

"Clifford…" she hesitated for a second. Taking a deep breath, she finished her piece. "Clifford, your mama died today."

"Impossible," I thought. I was getting ready to board a flight THAT DAY, to see her and say my good-byes. My sister, Melba, was already there, and other family members had gathered to be with mama. I was supposed to have a chance to say goodbye.

"I'm sorry." Evelyn tried to comfort me.

I turned and walked away, going into the backyard. I felt empty. Lost. Deep in my gut. Mama had always been there for me, through everything. I'd taken her support for granted. I took her presence for granted. And now she was gone.

I asked Evelyn to go with me to the funeral, but she refused. She had never felt accepted by members of my family, and didn't want to put herself in an uncomfortable situation. I didn't see it that way. I took it as yet another slap at me. My mama is dead, and you can't even stand by my side?

So I went by myself. I didn't stay long, leaving the day after the funeral. I needed to get the "heck outta dodge", though I wasn't coming home to any picnic. Evelyn and I were hitting the skids again, yet another back-breaking straw to add to the heap.

Intuitively, I knew Evelyn had reached her point of no return. My cocaine addiction reawakened the old Cliff, and Evelyn and the children's lives were wrapped in constant turmoil, anxiety and dishonesty, and she had had enough. I knew this, not from things she said, but through her behavior.

Our first time around, Evelyn would get upset, yell, scream, cry, and generally just be reactive to all the mess I got into. Now, she was as calm as a glassy sea. Never raising her voice. Never nagging me and hounding me about what I wasn't doing. Neither did she really acknowledge my existence. If I asked her to go to dinner, it was simply "No." If I asked her to do something else, "No."

With this last speck of stability slipping away, I let my frustration rip. If she didn't care about me anymore, fine. I aimed to hurt her as deep as I could—telling her everything I ever hated about her.

I blamed her for the drug mess I was in. If she had loved me and respected me, if she had let me be the man, if she had stuck by me and built me up instead of tearing me down, I never would have turned to drugs. All this was her fault, and I told her so. And through it all, she remained cool and calm. Completely unruffled. And that incensed me.

One day, I needed some money really bad. Not having anything to steal, not having a job, not having any other prospects for getting cash, I decided to ask Evelyn. She was at work, so I dialed her job.

"Hello?" She answered the phone in her business voice.

"Uh, Evelyn, this is Clifford."

"Uh huh."

"I was wondering… I uh, I need some money and I was wondering if you would spot me some cash."

"No."

"Come on Evelyn. I really need some cash. I'll pay you back."

"No."

"Dag Evelyn," my voice rose an octave as I continued to hit the brick wall she'd surrounded herself with. "I SAID I'll pay you BACK."

"The answer is still no, Clifford."

Regardless of what I said, Evelyn remained firm in her answer. She didn't allow herself to get drawn into a discussion or an argument. The answer was just "No." I grew more agitated by the second, until I couldn't handle her nonchalance any longer. I completely snapped.

"Who the do you THINK you are, acting like all that! You ain't nobody. YOU HEAR ME, EVELYN? If I saw you lying in some ditch, bleeding, I'D SPIT ON YOU AND KEEP ON GOING."

SLAM! The receiver cracked against the cradle as I

slammed the phone down. My blood raced a mile a minute. My head pounded like someone was knocking me over the head with a hammer. My breath came in short, hard bursts. How dare she dismiss me like I was nothing.

I knew it was over between Evelyn and me. The second time around had gotten worse than the first. What I didn't know, was that Evelyn had already filed for a divorce. I expected something to happen, knowing we were through. I actually said to her "don't you have no man comin' in here knockin' at the door, tellin' me 'Hey, you got 24 hours to go'." The same day I said that to Evelyn, she didn't come home that night.

The following day, I was holed up in the house, in the dark, doing cocaine. All the blinds were shut and the shades pulled down, and I was going for it. Suddenly, the doorbell rang. I ran to the window and peeked through the blind to see who it was. I recognized a detective's car in the front of the house.

Clifford, I thought to myself. *You might as well not prolong this, cause you know this is going to happen*. I opened the door just enough for me to see the man and him to see me.

"Mr. Clifford Harris?"

"Yes."

"These are for you." He handed me an envelope.

I shut the front door, and proceeded to open the envelope. Inside, the contents basically told me I had 24 hours to get out of the house. Furious, I called Evelyn's job. Once again, she met my nasty, filthy, cussing mouth with cool calmness.

"I can't believe you actually went ahead and did this mess, the very day after I told you not to." Her disregard for me and her defiance churned my insides.

"I did it, because it's time for you to go. You got to go, Clifford. I mean, I don't know why I married somebody with just a tenth grade education anyway."

I sucked my breath in like I'd just gotten sucker-punched in the gut and had the wind knocked out of me. Evelyn knew not finishing school was part of the core of my low self-esteem.

Well, that did it. I packed my bags and left the house, never to return to that life again. It was 1981.

————•————

I rented an apartment with Rick Owens, by high school buddy and drug partner, and my life continued to be an unending streak of drugs, stealing, and more drugs. Everyday. All day. Sometimes, I didn't even pay my half of the rent. I let everything go, except cocaine. Absolutely nothing else interested me. Cocaine was my all in all.

Sitting at the coffee table one day in my apartment, I was performing my drug ritual. I poured the cocaine onto a small mirror, and began chopping it into a fine powder with a razor blade. Intent on my task, I never noticed anyone enter the room.

"Hey, Cliff." A voice out of nowhere spoke my name, but I ignored it and kept on chopping.

"Hey! Cliff?" I kept on chopping, keeping my eyes intently on the coke.

"Clifford." That voice out of nowhere sounded a little more urgent. I just kept on chopping.

"CLIFFORD! LOOK AT ME."

I finally raised my eyes to see *Elvira, a girl who had been flirting with me off and on, posing in front of me without a stitch of clothes on. As naked as a jay bird. Without a second glance, I focused my eyes back to the table and kept on chopping.

I didn't need no woman, because cocaine was my lady. My "White lady."

————•————

*Name have been changed.

Finally, after about a year and a half my attempted burglary with Jerry, went to trial. No surprise to me, Jerry got probation, I got five years in the state penitentiary. That, in itself was very lenient. I'd expected life in prison because this was my third felony. It turned out, that wasn't the only break I got.

Waiting to go to prison, I heard rumors flying around that made my heart skip a beat, but I didn't want to get my hopes up. When I got the news straight from the prison itself, I wanted to leap into the air. The state penitentiaries were too full. To ease the overcrowding, nonviolent criminals were being sent to a halfway house operated by Colorado's penal system. That included me.

I was so psyched, I didn't know what to do. I wasn't going to prison after all. In the halfway house, I could live somewhat like a normal person. Best of all, I wouldn't be locked behind bars, suffocating in a putrid, matchbox cell.

As the magnitude of this lucky break sunk in, I began reflecting on all the circumstances that got me to this point. Woven in and out of those reflections were all the times my drug use nearly killed me. I had missed death by inches on so many occasions, they were almost too numerous to count. It was like a dance. A death dance.

*Listen to your father, who gave you life,
and do not despise your mother
when she is old.
Proverbs 23:22*

Chapter 16

DEATHDANCE

My first brush with death happened during early years of my heroin use. My partner, Ricky Owens, and I bought some super powerful heroin off the street. You could see this stuff was different, because it was black. Commonly, heroin is a white or brownish color. But this stuff was coal black.

"Oooo, I can't wait to try this junk," Ricky said excitedly. We were both salivating with anticipation of the high we were going to get with THIS dope.

Rushing home to Harris Mansion, we flew into the basement eager to cook it up and get our high on. I filled the syringe with my normal dosage and shot it into my vein. Within ten seconds I knew I had overdosed. All the air disappeared from the room and I couldn't breathe.

"Air, air," I mumbled, clasping at my throat. I had to get out of the basement so I could get some air. Stumbling up the stairs, clawing at my throat, I made it out the front door and fell like a domino—face down, flat on the ground.

I opened my eyes to see Ricky kneeling on the ground beside me, me now lying on my back. My body woke to feel his fists beating my chest, painful blow after blow, trying to revive me. My ears tuned up to hear him saying "Man, come on. DON'T DIE ON ME CLIFFORD. Come on, DON'T GIVE UP. You're going to be okay, man."

I stared, unblinking, straight into the sky, trying to focus. Ricky suddenly realized I was awake.

"Man, Clifford, you scared the mess outta me. I mean, you really scared me."

I turned my gaze to Ricky, and smiled.

"Maaan, let's go get some more of that stuff. Oooowee!, That's GOOD."

And off we went.

— — — — • — — — —

After my marriage to Evelyn ended the first time, I moved into a small house (that I shared with rats) down the street from my sister, Melba. I had no furniture, including a bed, so I slept on a cot. Despondent at losing my family, depressed about the way my life was going, I laid down on the cot to rest. Mellowed out on heroin, I lit a cigarette.

I came to, enveloped in a veil of thick smoke, coughing, sputtering, and totally disoriented. But it didn't take long to realize the mattress was on fire. Somehow, I managed to fight my way through the smoke and get out of the room. Again, God snatched me out of death's outstretched hands, but I always managed to find my way back.

— — — — • — — — —

In the early years, when I was trying to keep my drug use secret from my family, I often went to shooting galleries to do my business. In these places, drug addicts use and reuse the same needles. I'd find a needle lying on a coffee table. It usually had blood in the syringe from the last user. I'd simply put some water in, swish it around, then put my own drug in it and shoot it in my vein.

That's how addicts get AIDS and other communicable diseases; being exposed to other people's blood. But I didn't think about things like that. It wasn't important. Getting the drug into my system was my only concern.

Sometimes, those gallery needles would be so dull, one

would bend as I tried to stick it into my arm. Today, I bear two large scars on my arms where I stuck needles over and over again—permanent reminders of my life in hell.

———•———

During my on again, off again work relationship with Gage, there were periods where I went to work, stoned, all the time. Whenever my drug use escalated, I did not abstain during work hours so I could perform up to my skill level. I took drugs just to be able to function at all, and that included functioning on the job as well.

Not just the hard core stuff hampered my ability. Marijuana impaired me as well. In the time frame where I'd stopped using heroin for eight months, I retained my pleasure of smoking weed. I, and many other drug users, never put weed on the same level as heroin or cocaine, because it's not physically addicting. So to say, "I'm getting off drugs," never meant getting off weed.

One day I was working at a job site for Gage, way up in the mountains. Driving a forklift, I was going real slow (probably no more than three miles an hour) because I had been smoking weed on the job, one of the few times I did that. To guard against mishaps, I was being extra careful, especially since the steering wheel is in the back of the machine.

Now, the cab of a forklift is not very spacious, especially if one is a big person. I was wedged into the cab pretty tight, with no extra room available. Sitting high up off the ground, a big man like me can't jump in and out of the cab with ease. I had to maneuver in and out of the cab, climbing down to the ground and climbing back up.

While I maneuvered the forklift, that massive piece of machinery started veering off the road. Riding the edge of the road, the forklift tilted. Instantly the thought crossed my mind

"Clifford, you're gonna die." The machine began going down the side of the mountain, hitting rocks and other ground protrusions.

I couldn't jump out of the cab. My feet were too big to pull out, and if I did, I wouldn't successfully clear all the gears and gadgets in the way. As the forklift gathered speed, it bounced violently—enough to throw me off. I hit the ground and rolled.

I got up, dusted myself off, then proceeded to watch Gage's $20,000 forklift careen down the mountainside, flipping over boulders and crashing tree stumps. When it hit the bottom, the machine broke into little pieces.

Realizing how close I'd come to being dead, I was shaken. I walked to the place where I was living, and fired up some more weed to calm my nerves.

———•———

Ricky Owens and I were partners since meeting in high school. We became woven into the fabric of each other's lives, bonded through every experience we shared together. This, of course, included our introduction to and love affair with drugs. It was with Ricky I tried to kick my drug habit, and with Ricky, I stole to support it. But many times, drugs can make enemies out of your staunchest friends.

When Ricky and I were sharing an apartment, after I'd split with Evelyn the second time, we went out and copped some cocaine together. This was nothing new for us.

We poured the powder into a spoon, cooking it until it turned clear, just like water. If it did that, it meant the coke was pure. For whatever reason, Ricky walked away to do something, leaving me with the task of finishing the heating process. When I finished, I was supposed to draw half of the liquid into the syringe, leaving the other half in the spoon for Ricky.

In a fit of selfish pleasure, I drew all of the liquid into the syringe and shot it into my arm. I replaced what I'd taken with plain water. When Ricky came back, he drew up the water into the syringe, thinking it was his half of the cocaine, and shot it up. But nothing happened. Meanwhile, I was chillin' on the sofa, lying down, enjoying the effect of the drug.

Ricky silently left the room. He came back in, pistol in hand, leaned down and pulled the trigger. A bullet zoomed across the top of the first two fingers on my left hand, almost taking the tip of my index finger with it. Then, he turned and left the room.

If Ricky had gotten any closer, that bullet would have gone through my side, doing a heck of a lot more damage than it did. As a reminder of how drugs will take the place of human friends, one of my fingers is permanently bent at the first digit. A direct result of the day my friend tried to kill me.

———•————

Taking chances, no matter how stupid it seems, is par for the course when one's a drug addict. The only thing that is of any importance, is getting the drug. That's what I felt during one of my construction jaunts in Wyoming, working for Gage. I had no cocaine supplier in Wyoming, so if I wanted anything, I had to drive back to Denver—five hours away.

As the powerful craving pounded my senses, I knew I had to get to Denver to buy some relief. But the weather was terrible. We were in the midst of a bad snow blizzard, but was I going to let that stop me from making the trip? Hardly.

Friday night, after work, I got in my car and proceeded down the road, unable to see past the hood of the car. I inched down the 300 miles between Rock Springs and Denver, determined to get the supply of coke I needed to calm down. At one point, the Interstate closed. I sat for hours on the side of the road. When the snow let up a little and the plows came out, I headed onto the road again.

Never once did it enter my mind to turn around and go back to Rock Springs. I was on a mission, and I was not giving up until I had successfully accomplished what I set out to do. Ten hours later, I was finally in Denver. The trip had taken twice the normal time, but I didn't care.

I met up with George, my supplier, bought a good stash of coke, then jumped in the car and headed back. Since the Interstate was still closed, I used back roads, which created more problems. Most of the time, I drove in the middle of the road. More than once I had to push the car out of a snowbank.

None of this dangerous effort bothered me one bit. I had everything I needed right inside that car—water, a spoon, needles, and plenty of coke—a shooting gallery on wheels.

I arrived back in Rock Springs Sunday morning, around eleven o'clock. I had spent the entire weekend holed up in my car, foolishly battling a fierce snowstorm just to satisfy my insatiable cravings. But I was happy. I went home, slept, and went to work early Monday morning.

These are just a few incidences where God literally plucked me out of the grasp of Satan who was trying to snuff my life out. I didn't realize it then, but God wanted me alive. He had something very special planned for me. He just had to wait for me to lift the corner of the veil that darkened my mind.

The Lord said to Satan,
"The Lord rebuke you, Satan!
The Lord, who has chosen Jerusalem, rebuke
you! Is not this man a burning stick
snatched from the fire?
Zechariah 3:2

Chapter 17

FLICKER OF LIGHT

n my time of reflection, while waiting to be placed in the halfway house to fulfill my sentence, a startling thought hit me. The wrong turn my life had taken started with marijuana! Marijuana was the beginning of the end for me. The minute I gave into the temptation to smoke weed, I became vulnerable to trying bigger and better drugs.

That may seem like simple logic now. But then, it was a major revelation—particularly since I stopped smoking weed once I got into heroin, and then cocaine. The highs those drugs produced made using weed a joke.

To this day, I don't know why I made the decision, but I determined not to smoke any weed while I was doing my time. I didn't want it anywhere near me. That was a huge decision, because weed was the only drug readily available in prison. I knew I couldn't get any coke, but any and everybody had weed. And going to a halfway house, at that? Please, a decision to stop smoking weed altogether was akin to deciding to go straight.

The halfway house was like a small dormitory building. Inmates were assigned two to a room, and it housed males and females. The females lived downstairs, and the males upstairs. It had a common dining room, with regularly scheduled meals, and community bathrooms.

Inmates were allowed to leave the building, after saying where they were going, how long they were going to be wherever, when they were coming back, and signing out. Anyone leaving the premises had to sign back in before dark. Upon return to the residence, everyone had to submit to a urine drug test. Being drug free was a major stipulation for staying at the halfway house. Anyone caught using, was sent back to prison.

I held fast to my commitment not to smoke any weed, though the temptation was never-ending. Seems like every time I turned around, somebody was saying "Yo Harris, we got some good weed over here. Come on and get some." I'd just shake my head and decline the offer.

Once again, Gage came through for me and gave me a job working construction with him. That's the only place I went when I left the halfway house. But Gage didn't stop there. I still owned the Mustang he'd given me years ago, but I didn't have any insurance on it. The halfway house required that inmates who were car owners have insurance. Gage bought insurance for me so I could have transportation to and from work.

Each payday, I took my check to the bank and deposited it in my account. I was saving money, so when my sentence was finished, I could support myself. For some reason, the halfway house employees hated that—the fact that I had money and a bank account.

My job with Gage began in August. It seemed like that summer was one of the hottest I'd ever worked in, and August was no exception. The job site was in the middle of what used to be a cabbage field. Thus, there were absolutely no shade trees to shield us from the scorching sun. I labored everyday in the relentless heat, laying blocks for a huge building.

One evening when I returned to the halfway house, I submitted my urine sample, as usual, and waited for the result.

When the worker presented it to me, I was flabbergasted.

"You're positive, Harris."

Shaking my head from side to side, I protested. "That can't be right. I haven't taken anything."

"Uh, huh," he responded a little sarcastically. "The tests don't lie, Harris. You'd better get it together or you're gonna be outta here on your butt. You can be sure we'll be watching you like a hawk."

Incredulously, I went to my room. I really had not done any drugs, yet the drug count in my urine was high. It was really strange. And it didn't end there. Every time I came back from work, my urine sample was loaded with drugs, as if I'd spent all day puffing my head off. After each test, the dialogue was the same.

"You're still using, Harris? After we told you to cut it out?

"I'm not using. I swear."

"Right, Harris. You think I'm stupid? Your urine is loaded with stuff."

Well, something's wrong, cause I'm not doing anything. Why would I do that? You think I want to go back to prison. Come on. That would be crazy!"

"Then you're crazy, because the tests don't lie."

"Well I'm telling you, " I insisted, "I'm not doing anything. I go to work and come straight back here. That's all."

Each time we went through this, the man would look at me with this I-know-you're-lying look. And why wouldn't he? Addicts are skillful liars, so much so, you can never really be sure when they're telling the truth. If ever. Regardless, for the first few days the worker didn't do anything to me but reprimand me because I was so furiously pleading my innocence.

About the fourth day since all this started, the heat was so intense, Gage's crew knocked off the job early. It was too dangerous to keep working. My energy was so sapped by the heat we'd already endured, all I wanted to do was go to the halfway house and crash. Driving there, I suddenly felt a high coming on.

Huh. That's weird, I thought, blinking my eyes and rolling my head around. The sensation continued. *This is ridiculous.* My mind raced, trying to make sense of the unmistakable sensations I felt. *But its been weeks since I last did cocaine.*

I struggled to figure out what was happening to me. Was I blacking out and copping drugs at Five Points and doing them with no memory? No! I ain't crazy. I knew I wasn't unconsciously doing drugs, but I couldn't deny that I was definitely high. Needless to say, I stayed away from the halfway house. I needed some time to let this pass before submitting to a drug test.

It didn't do any good. When I returned that evening, my urine was loaded.

"Okay, that's IT Harris. I'm not letting you get by again. Expect to be up at four o'clock in the morning to wash all the walls in the house. Got it?"

"Yeah, I got it. But I didn't do any drugs." Disgusted, the worker disregarded my last statement. I was up the next morning washing walls.

A couple of nights later, I was watching the T.V. that Gage had given me, when I heard a knock at my door. I opened it to see the house supervisor standing there with a no-nonsense look on his face.

"You're outta here, Harris. Back to prison."

"What?" My mouth flew open in disbelief. "For WHAT?"

"Whatta ya mean, for what? For using. That's what."

"But I swear, I haven't touched anything since I've been here. Not even marijuana. NOTHING."

"Harris, you can deny it until you're blue in the face, but the tests don't lie. We know you're using, so you're going back to jail."

D—! I thought. *The ONE time I'm actually telling the truth and it doesn't get me anywhere but back in prison.* The frustration oozed from my pores, but it didn't make sense to keep protesting. They were not going to believe me. The inevitable was happening.

I ended back in the county jail, where I sat for two months before my case went to court. Once again, I tried to explain that I hadn't been using, but everyone kept pointing to the positive test results. All of the tests. All positive. Aside from that, they dealt with the person they knew I was—a twenty-year drug addict who'd been in and out of court maybe two hundred times or more. They didn't have one ounce of belief in my denial.

I went back to prison.

I sat in my cell, angry. I was back in this forsaken place, for nothing. My freedom lost, for nothing. And I couldn't even prove that I had done nothing. That was the infuriating part. I was actually innocent and had no shred of evidence to support it. I didn't even understand it myself.

After a couple of days, I calmed down. It was futile to keep tearing my insides up being angry for a situation that wasn't going to change. I was here, in prison, and would be here until I completed my sentence. *Just consider it pay back,* I thought *for all the other times you've done stuff and gotten away with it.*

That thought prompted what turned into deep self-reflection. All the other stuff I've done and gotten away with. All the stuff I've done that propelled me in and out of this penal system like a revolving door. All the stuff I've done to family and friends. My wife. My children. My parents. All the stuff I've done—drugs.

Drugs, I continued thinking. *"Drugs is at the bottom of everything. No matter what I pull up into memory, the common denominator is drugs. My addiction to drugs.*

Sitting in that cell, alone, I had to face the truth. Nobody was to blame for the way my life was, except me. *I'm 44 years old, sittin in this penitentiary for a second time, for what?* My thoughts continued cutting me like a razor. *For drugs.!*

My reflections marched on, replaying different scenarios along the path I'd chosen. What a waste. What an absolute waste. I'd missed so much. I had no one. Nobody trusted me as far as they could spit. My own mother had not wanted me around to see her when she was dying. But who could I blame? Nobody but me. And again, drugs was at the bottom of it all.

I'm tired, I thought. *I'm tired of this life—the police, being in and out of jail, using drugs and withdrawing from drugs and using drugs again, getting beat out of my money from other addicts. The whole thing. I'm tired of everything.* Suddenly, another thought occurred to me. *So, stop the drugs. Not just weed. All of it.*

Sounds simple. Sounds like I could have thought of that years ago, and I did. But I wasn't ready to make a truthful commitment until now. *If I stop the drugs,* I reasoned with myself, *I won't ever have to come back to this place again. EVER.* The penal system was going to have to let me go, and once it did, I'd have to never set foot in it again. The choice was mine. And finally, I made it.

Of course, my first test in prison came just hours after I had this conversation with myself.

"Yo, Harris." An inmate I knew to be a heavy drug user came to my cell. "We got some weed over here." He pointed to three men standing off to the side. "Come on and join us. We can do it together."

"No thanks."

"NO. What you mean no thanks."

"I'm not interested. I don't want any." Laughing, the man didn't accept my simple refusal.

"Aw come on Harris, we know you."

"I said no man, that's the reason I'm in here now. So forget it. I'm not doing it anymore."

"Puhlease, Harris," the guy rolled his eyes. "We both know the minute you get outta here, you gonna be down at Five Points copping some stuff. So don't even try to play that game with me."

"We'll see," I responded, then turned and walked away.

The inmate's assessment of me made me more determined to stick to my decision. Who did he think he was, acting like he knew me so well? He didn't know me, and I was going to prove it.

As the days passed, reflections continued streaming in and out of my head. One logical thought led to another logical thought. I began thinking about church, and it hit me—*people who go to church don't go to jail.* In that case, going back to church would have to be step two in my plan to never return to jail. *When I get out of here, I'm going to church.*

During this period, I never attributed my self-reflections to spiritual prompting. I wasn't aware of God and his awesome power. I'd left thoughts about God back in my childhood days. All I felt I was doing, was making logical, right decisions. But as I look back, now, I know that God's spirit was moving on my heart; clearing my head to be able to think things through logically.

The same day I decided to start going to church once I got

out of prison, I went to the prison library. I enjoyed looking at the female librarian, (not because she was attractive, because she wasn't) just because she was a woman. In jail, we rarely saw any women, and any opportunity we inmates had to be around one, we took it.

I realized, though, I couldn't just sit in the library staring at her, so I started browsing the shelves looking at books. I stopped cold—riveted by a title wedged between the other books on the shelf. *The Desire of Ages* was a book I remembered being in my parents' house. It was a book on the life of Jesus. Flashbacks of me as a child listening to my parents read passages from that book, filled my very being. I smiled and hurt at the same time—realizing how pleasant those days were, and missing my childhood and family.

I carried the book up to the counter and checked it out. Back in my cell, I put *The Desire of Ages* on my table. It sat there, unopened, until the date it was due back in the library. On the due date, I renewed the book, and sat it on my table. Again, I never opened it. It was enough just to stare at the picture of Jesus on the cover, reminiscing about days long gone.

I kept renewing *The Desire of Ages* and staring at it as it adorned the table. Something was happening to me. I didn't pray; I didn't think about reading the Bible. Yet, just having that book in my presence induced a cleansing process I'd never experienced.

I couldn't look at the book without seeing myself as a child experiencing the spiritual upbringing that bonded my family together and kept us secure. I couldn't look at that book without remembering church, and Sabbath, and dinner with aunts and uncles and cousins. I couldn't look at that book without realizing that when I had all those other things—family, church, Sabbath, Jesus—my life was good. Once I let them go, my life disintegrated.

Utter shame overwhelmed me as I acknowledged what I'd become. I preyed on everyone I'd ever loved. I was not fit to be a husband or father. I'd trampled over Evelyn and each of the children, robbing myself of any chance of a meaningful life with Stephen, Jeffrey and Rhonda.

I was not fit to be a son or brother. I'd abused my parents' unconditional love for me—conning them out of money, dragging them into the mess of my life, begging them to rescue me from the law. I didn't even know my brothers and sisters anymore, or know their children. They all kind of kept me at arms length, unwilling to trust me.

I wasn't fit to be a member of my extended family—all the aunts, uncles, and cousins I'd grown close to as a child. Nobody had anything to do with me, once I succumbed to my drug addictions. Some of them had died without me ever seeing them again. I could never renew those relationships.

Overwhelmed with grief, I cried. The magnitude of the pain and hurt my loved ones experienced at my hands, wrenched my soul. I had destroyed more than I could ever hope to rebuild. A despairing reality. After the tears, though, another reality lingered. All I had done in the past, was yesterday. There was nothing I could do to change that. But I could make changes today, and tomorrow offered the promise of newness.

And therein, lies the difference between previous times I'd beaten myself up for ruining lives, and what I was experiencing in that jail. I began to forgive myself. I didn't hold on to the demons accusing me of being a failure, a rotten person, a no-good addict. When I did that, I used drugs to escape—to "build" myself back up. This time, I accepted responsibility for my actions, but determined to be different today and tomorrow. One day at a time.

That principle has not changed. Today, there are events I cannot recount without sobs choking the words in my throat, tears coursing down my cheeks. I will always hurt when I realize how evil I treated those I loved. But I walk around that pain in the knowledge that I am forgiven.

Gradually my head cleared and the picture became razor sharp. I knew exactly what Cliff had to do to reclaim his life. And the process had already begun.

For I know the plans I have for you,"
declares the Lord,
"plans to prosper you and not to harm you,
plans to give you hope and a future.
Then you will call upon Me and come and
pray to Me, and I will listen to you.
You will seek Me
and find Me
when you seek Me with all your heart."
Jeremiah 29:11-13

Chapter 18

NEW LIFE

The days neared the end of my prison stay. I was being paroled, meaning I didn't have to complete the entire five years of my sentence. Counting the hours, I started thinking about what I was going to do once I was released. Before release, the prison made inmates fill out all kinds of forms, and one thing they had to know was where you planned to live.

To keep my commitment of staying drug free, I knew I couldn't go back to anything that was familiar. If I was really changing, I had to change everything, including my environment. I thought about Melba, to whom I'd sent my clothes when I left the halfway house. I decided to call her.

"Hello?" The voice belonged to one of my nieces.

"Hey sweetie. Is your mama there?"

"Hold on." I could hear her in the background say "It's Uncle Cliff." After a few moments, I heard another extension pick up.

"I love you." My sister's voice rang firm and clear as she uttered those three little words. She didn't even say "hello" or "how are you." She got on the phone and said "I love you." Instantly, tears of shame filled my eyes. Here was someone I had misused—stealing things from her and her husband to finance my drug habit—and the first thing she does is say she loves me? Here is an example of how I consistently slapped down those who loved me the most, yet she says she loves me?

I barely choked through the words of apology for the numerous times I did her and her family wrong. I didn't bother to tell her of the decisions I'd made to change. It sounded empty and superficial. I'd said that so many times before, it was like crying "wolf." No, I wouldn't mention that—I'd have to show her that I'd changed. I did ask if I could stay with her once I was released from prison.

"Sure you can, Clifford." She didn't hesitate, or come up with a slew of reasons why that wasn't feasible. Just, "sure."

I walked back to my cell, humbled by the kindness and love Melba extended to me. For the first time, I felt a sense of hope that my life was truly going to be different, and it made me feel alive.

I was released on parole, Sunday morning, January 1984. As I walked through the gate, the guard said, "Hey Harris, see you in about six months."

"We'll see," was the answer I threw over my shoulder as I walked toward the street. Just like the inmate who said I'd be back on drugs, the guard's words made me more determined to prove them all wrong.

"Cliff. Hey, Cliff."

I looked toward the car where the voice was coming from.

Inside, I saw Jerry—my friend who had talked me into the attempted burglary that landed me in prison.

"Hey man, what are you doing here?" I peeped inside his car.

"Hop on in, man. I came to pick you up; take you wherever you need to go."

I don't know how Jerry knew I was getting out on that day, but his unrequited gesture showed he hadn't forgotten me.

"Thanks man. I appreciate it."

Jerry drove me to Melba's house, where she had a little room in the basement ready and waiting for me. Melba and I hugged real tight, ecstatic to see each other again. Shaking Ed's hand I thanked both of them profusely for allowing me to stay there. I never expected, though, to be served a huge slice of humble pie. When I received it, I had to eat without complaint.

"Clifford, turn out the lights", "Clifford, turn down your radio", "Clifford, be back in the house by 12 midnight." My sister didn't lack for house rules and regulations, and I was expected to abide by them like anybody else. Didn't matter that I was 44 years old, and not 10. I was under their roof and had to respect their rules.

Looking back now, the structure and discipline were good for me. I never resented Melba and Ed for their parental treatment. I was totally grateful to them for allowing me into their home. But I did feel more like a child than a man, and in some ways, I guess I still was a child. It was humbling, but I took it because I had to. I had made a commitment to change, and this was part of the deal.

———•———

On Monday, I decided to pay a visit to an old friend.

"Hey Chief," I glibly addressed the man standing in the office. Gage Behunin turned to see me standing there.

"Hello, Clifford."

On my way to Gage's office I was positive he'd give me a job. But now I wasn't so sure. His attitude toward me was a little different than I was used to. Somewhat cold and aloof. And why wouldn't it be? Here was another person who'd treated me so well and who I repaid with evil. I felt a little uneasy, but it didn't stop me from making my request.

"Look Chief, I need a job."

"Sorry Clifford. I don't have any bricks for you to lay."

"That's okay. You can give me anything to do," I said accommodatingly. "I just want to work."

Gage looked at me a few seconds, as if trying to judge my sincerity.

"Okay. You can walk around the job site and clean up the bathrooms, sweep up the debris, and clean whatever else you see that needs cleaning."

"No problem, Chief. I really appreciate the work."

I happily took the mop and bucket and got started. I determined that Gage would have the cleanest job site around. I didn't care if I looked like a maid. I didn't care that he was paying me $5 an hour, when he used to pay me $25 an hour for laying bricks. All that mattered, was that I was drug free and I had a job. I knew I had to prove myself to him. I'd hurt Gage so many times, and his willingness to give me a small crumb was still an extended hand.

Gage had taken the car back he'd given me, when I left the halfway house and went back to prison. So every day, I took the bus from one side of Denver to the end of the line, where I walked another three miles to work. I didn't complain. I actually enjoyed sight-seeing and breathing the fresh air. Those little things mean a lot when one's been locked up in a jail cell. Besides, I was just grateful to have a job to go to .

My first Saturday home, Melba and I were sitting at the breakfast table.

"Clifford," Melba began, "are you going to church?"

"No, I ain't going to no church." Even as I said the words, I knew I was reneging on the second promise I'd made myself while in prison. But I had a good excuse, so I thought.

"I don't want all those people asking me a bunch of questions "'Where you been? What you been doing?'" I just don't want to deal with that."

"Okay." Melba left it at that, and got up from the table to

get dressed.

Sitting there by myself, I thought about the church. It was where my family had put our membership when we moved to Denver in my teens. Many old members, still there, knew my family, and probably already knew what I'd been doing all the years I'd been gone. I didn't want to face their stares and comments.

Gradually, I became aware of a small voice speaking to me. A voice I had tuned out a long, long time ago.

"Clifford," it said, *"remember when you were in that cell? You wished you were in church. You wanted to be at prayer meeting. You wanted to be in Sabbath School. Well, now is your chance. If you don't take this chance, you're going to die."*

I was dressed and ready for church in five minutes.

Melba and Ed had already left, so I walked to church. That small voice kept talking to me.

"Clifford, you know all those times you've almost died? You know all those times you should have gotten caught doing what you were doing, and you didn't? You know all those times people deserted you and didn't want to have anything to do with you? I've been the One protecting you. I've been the One watching over you. I've been the One whose never left your side."

I didn't respond to what I was hearing. I just listened and walked.

"Well, now's the time Clifford. Now's the time to make a decision to be with Me, or against Me. You can't decide tomorrow, or next week, or even an hour from now. You have to decide now."

God was finally giving me an ultimatum. He'd waited for me twenty years, watching me "live" life my way. Now, I had to make a decision to *live* life His way. Right then I decided in His favor. Once I made my decision to be with Him, my commitment was tested from the very beginning.

When I stepped foot into the church, the first member I saw was an elderly woman who'd known me since I was a teenager. She stared at me in horrified shock.

"What are YOU doing here?"

Nearly rolling my eyes in disgust, I managed to control my annoyance at what I perceived to be her judgment of me. Who did she think she was? She didn't know me or anything about my life.

"I'm doing the same thing you're doing, here." With that, I just walked past her into the church sanctuary.

Sitting in the back, the small voice kept speaking to me, telling me *I was where I had to be. It didn't matter that I was uncomfortable and self-conscious. It didn't matter what people knew or thought or might say about me. I had to stay, or I would die.*

I didn't get anything out of the Sabbath School lesson, nor anything out of the sermon. People didn't talk to me, and I didn't go out of my way to talk to them. Just being in church was enough for me, right then. And every time the church doors opened for a service, I was there. Sabbath services, Adventist Youth Society meetings on Sabbath afternoon, Wednesday night prayer service, evening meeting on Sunday. It didn't matter. I needed that spiritual foundation if my life changes were going to last.

Gradually in the following weeks, church members began greeting me when I walked through the door. Soon, a few were stopping and engaging in small conversation with me.

About the third or fourth week since I'd started going to church, I was sitting in a Sabbath School class, when I heard a voice directed at me.

"Clifford Harris!" I turned to see a woman named Joan,

rushing toward me. She threw her arms around me in an enthusiastic hug.

"It's so good to see you here. How are you?"

She sat beside me and we chatted a few minutes. We'd known each other as teenagers in that same church. Joan didn't pry into my business or treat me like a leper. She made me feel like I belonged at that church, and I will never forget her for that.

Joan died in the early '90s, leaving a huge imprint on my heart. Her embrace of me into the church family came at a time when I really needed somebody to care. To this day, I am grateful.

————•————

Evelyn knew I was out of the penitentiary, and she forbade the children to make contact with me. She was bitterly angry with me, and I couldn't blame her. My relationship with Stephen, Jeffrey and Rhonda ended when I went back to prison, so I hadn't seen or even talked to them in a few years.

Jeffrey was the only one still going to church, and he was a member of the same church I returned to. I'm sure he heard through the grapevine I'd been released from prison. One Friday, after I'd just gotten home from work, Jeffrey made a surprise visit.

I don't know how he found out I was staying with Melba, but he did.

"Daddy," he gushed, giving me a bear hug. "How are you doing?"

My heart swole up as I looked at Jeffrey. He'd grown into a handsome man, who was still moving on doing something with his life.

"Does your mother know you're here?"

Shaking his head, Jeffrey said, "No. She wouldn't like it if she knew I came to see you, and I'd rather not hurt her."

I understood and didn't say anything else about it. Jeffrey filled me in on what Stephen and Rhonda were doing. I also knew Jeffrey was in college, and asked how it was going.

"Well, I'm having a little money trouble right now." He proceeded to share the financial difficulties he was having. His sharing gave me the opportunity to feel like a real dad, a feeling I hadn't experienced in several years.

"How much do you need?" I asked Jeffrey.

"About $250 dollars."

I pondered for a moment, then I made a gesture that surprised, even me.

"Here." I held my hand out to Jeffrey. In it was my entire paycheck. I had worked a lot of extra hours that week and the check totaled just a little more than what Jeffrey needed. He stared at it, aghast I even had any money.

"Here. Go on, take it." I pushed my hand toward him, encouraging him to take the check. "You need it more than I do. Just consider it a very small token for all the times I didn't help you."

As my son hugged me, tears flowed down my cheeks. *This,* I thought to myself, *is what being a father is all about. Helping out my son.*

Melba's house rules were getting harder and harder to stomach as the months rolled by. I never displayed a negative attitude about it. I just knew I needed to get my own place as soon as possible.

I was saving all my money to do just that when, after about three months, Gage's son, Donny, gave me some money to rent my own place. About that same time, Gage took away my mop and pail and put me to work under Glen, his superintendent and carpenter. After about two weeks, Gage gave me a job laying bricks at an apartment complex he was refurbishing.

I was still walking three miles to work from the bus station. I didn't know it, but Gage's wife, Barbara, saw me walking to work one day. I also didn't know that she'd approached Gage about it. "Why don't you give him the car back," she'd questioned. "Hasn't he proved himself enough, already?" The next day, Gage gave me back the car. All these wonderful blessings God rewarded my commitment with, didn't negate the tests I still endured.

Though I had given up drugs, I still smoked cigarettes while in prison. Increasingly, I'd grown concerned about church members being able to smell tobacco on my breath and my clothes. I didn't want to be tied to chewing a bunch of gum, or spraying myself down before I went to church. Besides, if I was going to be a practicing Seventh-day Adventist, that included giving up smoking. So I decided to quit. Cold turkey.

Of course, each time I made a decision to change something, Satan always threw it in my face. Seems like the minute I decided to stop smoking, he paraded people in front of me who were smokers. Guys on the job would have cigarettes dangling from their mouths, and I'd breathe in the fumes, longing to have "just one."

Many times I came close to bumming a cigarette off somebody, but each time I sent up a prayer asking God for the strength to resist. Each time I passed a test, the next one was a little less difficult.

I was working alone repairing bricks on the windows and steps at the apartment complex Gage was remodeling. This required that I get behind the thick hedges growing around the building.

This one day, I pulled back the bushes from a window to check the brick. I stopped dead in my tracks. Sitting on the window sill was a brand new, unopened pack of cigarettes. My brand! Not just any brand. But the brand I used to smoke.

The first thing that ran through my head was *you can have one of them. Nobody's gonna know.* But I would know. I was trying hard to get my spiritual life together and I didn't want to half step. I wanted to do it right. I wanted to be for real. I wanted to be honest. Not so much for other people, but for myself.

"Oh no, no, no devil," I said aloud. "You not faking me out anymore. You've faked me out for twenty years, but not this time." I reached out, grabbed the pack of cigarettes and just twisted the whole pack around. Then, I threw them away.

By my birthday in January of 1985, one year since my release, I hadn't missed a single Sabbath at church. I hadn't officially rejoined as a member, but I had grown in my spiritual understanding. More important to me than joining the church, was building my relationship with God—understanding that He loved me so much, that He willingly died for me; accepting the fact that He'd forgiven me for all the crap I'd done in the past.

Even though I'd heard all this over and over from my parents during my childhood, I didn't understand it until now, at age 45. I didn't understand it, until I experienced it for myself.

————•————

To facilitate my change of direction, I had to sever ties to anything that reminded me of my former life. That meant I couldn't go to the same places I used to go, hang with the same people I used to hang with, or conduct anything in my life the way I used to.

As a result, I never went down to Five Points after my release. I never called any of my buddies. And I packed away my interest in women. I had used women my entire life for different reasons—to fill a void, to build my self-esteem, and to get what I wanted. If I was going to be different, I had to change my focus and get myself together.

I developed a single-track mind, never giving into the temptation to be social or date any of the attractive women in the church. I needed to stay focused on God and what we were trying to accomplish. I didn't have the ability to do that while getting involved with females. I also didn't want to give myself any opportunities to be trapped by old habits.

The first Sabbath in February of 1985, Jeffrey and I were standing in the church lobby having a conversation. Through the doors breezed an attractive, light-skinned woman who zipped right past me and stopped at Jeffrey.

"Jeffrey!" she exclaimed, kissing him on the cheek. "How are you doing? I haven't seen you for a couple of weeks."

Watching this encounter, I couldn't stop staring at the woman's face. My normal habits would have involved checking out her legs and everything else about her body, but her face riveted me. It wasn't because she was physically beautiful. But her face radiated such peace. Her voice rang joyful, and her whole person exuded happiness.

"She's the one."

I heard the voice so clearly in my head. As clear as if someone was standing next to me, saying it in my ear. Confused, I resisted the voice. I had purposely stayed away from getting involved with women. Yet, this voice was telling me this woman was THE one? I continued staring at her as she talked with Jeffrey. Intuitively, I felt she had the kind of relationship with Jesus that I envied.

When they finished talking, the woman went into the church sanctuary.

"Who is that?" I asked Jeffrey.

"Oh, that's Freddie, daddy." Jeffrey eyed me. "Do you want to meet her?"

"No, no, not now." Jeffrey looked at me, grinning.

"Yeah, you do."

Before I could stop him, Jeffrey walked into the church sanctuary and came back with Freddie in tow.

"Dad, this is Freddie. Freddie, this is my dad, Clifford Harris." The pride in Jeffrey's voice was unmistakable and hard to miss. I felt like bursting out in tears.

"Hi," Freddie said.

"Hi," I answered. Not thinking of anything else to say, I just stood there, awkwardly. I am known as someone who can run his mouth, but at this particular time, I was quiet.

"You have a wonderful son," she said, putting her hand on Jeffrey's shoulder. "You should feel very proud of him. I'm kind of like a second mother to Jeffrey. I hope you don't mind."

All I could do was smile. I didn't even answer her.

"Well," she continued, "they're getting ready to start. Why don't we go inside."

I followed her into the sanctuary, wondering what major change my life was headed for this time.

Freddie wasn't at church the following Sabbath. But I saw her at youth meeting that afternoon. I was standing in the lobby when she walked in. When our eyes met, I smiled.

"Hi," she said walking over to me. My grin got much wider.

"Hi," I returned her greeting. Then without even thinking about it, I said "I'm looking for a Christian friend. Would you like to be that friend?" The minute the words left my lips I was nervous. What had I just done? This woman knew absolutely nothing about me. What a dumb thing to ask.

"I think I'd like that."

I almost did a double take, not expecting to hear that

response.

We talked for a few more minutes, then we exchanged telephone numbers and made a date for the next day. When we parted, I couldn't get Freddie out of my head. I didn't know how I was going to last until Sunday without seeing her. As it turned out, I couldn't.

Saturday evening I called Freddie.

"I know our date isn't until tomorrow," I began, after greeting her, "but I was wondering, could I come over now? I have something to give you."

Puzzlement resounded in Freddie's voice as she responded,

"You have something for me? You don't even know me." But I did know her. I knew enough to know that I wanted to be around her because she would bring another level of spirituality to my life. Besides, the voice told me she was THE one.

"I do know you," I countered. Freddie hesitated a little.

"Come on over, then."

That's all I needed. I jumped in my car and zipped to Freddie's house before she had an opportunity to think about what was happening. This whole friendship was going lightening fast. Apparently, we both had positive intuitions about each other and could not fight the pull we felt toward each other.

Standing on Freddie's porch, I felt like a high-school boy waiting to go on his first date. When Freddie opened the front door, I held out my hand to her. In it, was a single, long-stemmed red rose.

"This is for you."

She was quite taken aback, but her face glowed as she smiled the broadest smile I'd ever seen.

"Oh Cliff, it's beautiful. Thank you. Come on in."

She ushered me into her house, and we sat down. I'd barely

been there a few minutes before we heard stomping steps coming from the basement up the stairs. Shortly, Freddie's eight-year old son emerged through the door and into the room where we were sitting. He was upset his older brother and sister had kicked him out of the basement where they were entertaining their friends, and he was tattling to his mother. When he saw me, he hopped up into my lap.

"That's okay," I assured him. "You can join our party."

Freddie and I proceeded to talk for about three hours. I discovered Freddie worked as the Bible instructor for our church, a person who gives Bible studies to non-believers and works closely with the church pastors. She also worked as a colporteur, going from door to door in different neighborhoods selling Christian books and magazines.

The conversation was so easy and comfortable, like we'd been old friends for a long time. I knew if this relationship was going to be THE one, I'd have to come clean about my past. But I didn't want to do it right then.

"I have something I need to talk to you about, tomorrow." My voice was a little serious. Freddie's facial expression took on my tone. "It's very important," I continued, "and I want you to hear it from me, rather than anybody else."

"Okay."

"Can you meet me at my place, tomorrow? It would be better if we didn't have any interruptions."

"Sure. I can do that."

"Great."

I finally had to pull myself away from Freddie and bring the evening to a close. Saying our good-byes, I left for home, ecstatic at the success of the evening. Nothing I feared would happen as a result of my calling so fast, happened. It would be hard waiting for tomorrow.

The next day Freddie met me at my house about noon. Inside, we sat on opposite ends of the couch. I was a little apprehensive about her reaction to what I was going to share. I knew if she had any problem with it—any problem whatsoever—our relationship could not go any further.

"Freddie," I began, "I want to tell you about me and the kind of life I lived, up until last year. I wanted you to get it straight from the horse's mouth, so you'd know what's truth and what's gossip."

"Okay. Tell me."

And I did. I didn't leave one, sordid detail out. I didn't try to hide anything. I didn't try to gloss anything over. I didn't try to make myself look good. I just told her straight. When I finished, I fell silent, waiting for her response.

"Is that all?" she asked.

"Yes." I looked right into Freddie's eyes. She held my gaze. When she didn't make any other remarks, I asked simply, "Will you marry me?"

"Yes."

My heart flew to the ceiling, it leapt so high for joy. She actually said "yes." It was easy for me to propose to Freddie because of the kind of woman she was, the life she led. But for her to say "yes" so readily? It was hard to understand, until she told me that the same small voice I'd heard two weeks earlier telling me Freddie was THE one, had said the same thing to her about me.

For the first time, we made physical contact. I took her into my arms and kissed her. She was the crowning touch to my new life. We set a date for April 26, 1985. We started making plans for a traditional church wedding. But, as we discovered, getting married wasn't the breeze we assumed it would be.

When we made the announcement individually to our

respective family and friends, it ignited a firestorm. Friends of Freddie's, as well as many church members, warned her she was making a big mistake marrying an ex-drug addict. People who'd known me since my teens, sought to protect her from me. Some vigilante church officials pronounced our plans to marry, non-biblical because of my past marital history.

On my side, Melba expressed concern about the rapidity with which this was happening. Fully aware of my track record and past habits, she thought I should slow things way down.

Needless to say, everyone's opinions planted seeds of doubt in both our minds, at different times. Each time, we'd talk them out, go our separate ways and pray about it, then come back together with renewed faith that we were doing the right thing.

In the middle of this mess, I got rebaptized into my church—this same church where some people were busy denigrating my character. But they didn't bother me. I couldn't let them decide my soul's salvation. My Christian walk was between God and me, and now, Freddie. All the callous statements of how I hadn't really changed made me more determined than ever to prove everybody wrong.

Eventually, the firestorm blew up in our faces. After 200 wedding invitations were mailed out, we canceled our church wedding. Things had really turned ugly, but we didn't let it discourage us. We were determined that our marriage would become a reality. We both knew, it was where God was leading us.

One weekend in May, we drove to Oklahoma City to visit some of Freddie's family. A nephew was getting married May 11, and we drove Freddie's mom, who had been visiting us in Denver. Many were aware of our situation, and annoyed at the turn of events.

"Listen Freddie," her sister-in-law said, "this isn't right. You guys are going to get married. There's no reason why you should have to wait."

Before we could blink, plans went into action. Freddie's sister-in-law, who was a nurse, got us to a clinic where we had blood tests completed in ten minutes. We went to the courthouse to get a marriage license, then the sister-in-law escorted us to the office of a former schoolmate, who was now a judge. He was just leaving for lunch, when she stopped him.

After preliminary greetings and introductions, she asked, "We want you to marry Cliff and Freddie. Will you do it?"

"Sure. I'm happy to do it."

Standing in our matching tee-shirts and jeans, we looked a far cry from the picture-perfect bride and groom we'd planned to be. No elegant wedding dress for Freddie. No tux for me. No bridesmaids or groomsmen. But we had love, and plenty of it.

Freddie and I were married in Oklahoma City on May 10, 1985. We did it a second time at a Denver courthouse, June 10. Unfortunately, the firestorm didn't end with our marriage, but my new life was cemented. In Jesus, and in Freddie.

Therefore, rid yourselves of all malice and all deceit, hypocrisy, envy, and slander of every kind. Like newborn babies, crave pure spiritual milk, so that by it you may grow up in your salvation, now that you have tasted that the Lord is good.
1 Peter 2:1-3

Chapter 19

REACHING BACK

t's very stressful being a drug addict. Day in and day out, I had nothing to strive for other than to figure out where my next fix was coming from, or how I was going to get the cash to get that fix. I was always looking over my shoulder to make sure the cops weren't going to bust me, or the next drug addict wasn't going to cheat me, or the people I conned weren't going to kill me.

I used to hate to see the night come, because that meant a new day was starting and I had nothing. No direction. No goals. No inspiration. And nothing to show for the end of the day, except an empty feeling. Everyone else was coming home after a hard day's work, having accomplished something constructive. And all I had to show for the day, was emptiness.

Now, with the change in my life, I was experiencing a high I'd never known. A high that stayed with me twenty-four-seven, and didn't cost a dime. What was that high? Peace of mind. Even more important than church, or Freddie—peace of mind. To this day, that has remained the most valuable result of my life's change. The Lord lifted me out of living the drug life, I wanted to help others find this peace of mind.

Ironically, I had my first thought of helping others while on a mad hunt for drugs one day. I had money—for once—and I was rushing to and fro trying to find someone to cop from. That day, it seemed like nobody had anything. But I refused to stop until I found somebody to sell me what I needed.

Once satisfied, I headed down Seventeenth Street—a huge, wide street in Denver, adorned on either side by rich, lavish homes. I was flying down the street when a thought crossed my mind. All this energy I used today to find these drugs, if I could turn that energy around for the positive—like helping somebody not go through all this stuff I just went through, and go through everyday—what a force I'd be.

Finally, I was ready to put energy into doing just that—helping other addicts achieve peace of mind and a new life. But I had to reach back into my own family, first, and help someone I'd dogged my entire life.

When Mama died, Daddy lived alone, caring and providing for himself in the house where they'd lived together. As senility began creeping in, one of Daddy's brothers, who'd promised Mama he would look after him, took him into his family and cared for him.

Shortly after marrying Freddie, I took her to Jacksonville, Florida to meet my father. He hadn't known about my conversion, so he had no idea of the new direction I was moving in. We had a wonderful time during our visit, the best time I'd had with my dad in years. We actually enjoyed ourselves without any mess spoiling the gathering.

Before Freddie and I left to return to Denver, my uncle called me in for a little conversation.

"Clifford, I can see you have really changed."

"No, I haven't done anything. God has changed me."

"Well, it's clear to see it's for real and I'm happy for that. And because it's real, I want you to take your father."

I stared at my uncle, slightly disbelieving what he'd just suggested. I loved my father dearly, but I wasn't sure I could care for him properly. Even though he'd succumbed to the first signs of senility, he wasn't totally helpless. He was still strong and persistent, and I was still his son.

"I'm not so sure that's a good I idea," I responded.

"Why not? He needs to be around his children, in a familiar area. I think moving to Denver would be good for him, and you're the perfect choice."

All kinds of reasons why I wasn't the "perfect choice" ran through my head. I'm not sure I could take Daddy treating me like a little boy. I was a newlywed. How would Freddie feel having to share the responsibility for caring for my aging father? On and on I thought, coming up with several reasons why he shouldn't live with me.

But in the end, we did move Daddy to Denver to live with us, because it was the right thing to do. And what a full circle.

More than once, Daddy looked at me and commented incredulously, "Clifford, I never dreamed. I never dreamed that you would be the one taking care of me. Just think of it. Out of all my children, who would have thought you—the one who caused me the most trouble—would be the one?"

Yes, who would have thought? And it was the best thing I could have ever done. What perfect closure to the gulf that separated me from my parents, that my father would be able to experience a relationship with me, devoid of evil. We talked often of my childhood and many times he'd say reassuringly

"You know, Clifford, your mother never stopped loving you."

On occasion, when I worked jobs for Gage, he invited Daddy to come along and sort of revisit the glory days when Daddy and I worked side by side way back when. My elderly father really couldn't do much, but Gage made him feel good by making him feel needed. What compassion that showed for the man, and the kind of employee, my dad used to be.

I thank God I was given six years with my father before he

died in 1992, at the age of 95.

———•———

Whenever I had the opportunity to talk with drug addicts, I jumped on it. God had been performing so many miracles in my life, I wanted everybody to know the joy they could have just by turning their lives over to Him. But talking to people individually and sporadically, didn't seem like enough.

Freddie and I prayed for an opportunity to share my story with many people at one time. We decided to take a stab at the Rocky Mountain News to see if they'd be interested in printing an article about my redemption from drugs. To our amazement, they sent a writer, with photographer, who wrote a two-page article published in the newspaper.

On the Sabbath after the article appeared, a gentleman approached me after services.

"I was impressed with the article I read about you in the paper, and I wanted to meet you."

Holding out my hand, I shook his and thanked him for his kind words. In the short conversation that followed, I felt impressed to give him my business card. Handing it to him I said, "Call me, if you ever need anything." He took the card appreciatively, and walked away.

The very next day, I was surprised to hear his voice on the phone.

"About ten years ago," he informed me, "I used to be a member of your church."

"No kidding." I was amazed at the instant connection.

"But I've been a cocaine addict, and I'm at my lowest point, ever. You've been where I am and you got out. I need you to help me."

Those were the best words I ever heard. What a thrill to know this man felt I could help him, after reading my story in the paper. That was exactly the response I hoped the article would generate.

I went to visit him, sharing and discussing our common experiences. Eventually, I witnessed the man's own redemption from drugs and his rebaptism into our church. My small involvement with this man prompted discussions between Freddie and me on some kind of ministry for drug addicts. "I can't just walk away," I often said. "I want to help them change and experience what I'm experiencing."

We collected information on becoming a nonprofit company, but with neither of us being college educated, we just didn't know how to go about putting a formal ministry together. For months, we did nothing. Finally, we created a support group for addicts desiring to be rid of their habits, but it didn't really get off the ground. Little did Freddie or I know that Denver was not to be home base for our ministry.

Through a series of events orchestrated through spiritual providence, Freddie and I relocated to California. It was there we created and birthed DAP (Drug Alternative Program), inspired by the many people who approached me wherever I shared my story, with their own stories of children, siblings, or friends who were currently battling drug addiction.

DAP began as a support group for drug dependents and co-dependents. We started with two people(a couple where the husband was drug dependent and on probation from jail—meeting on Saturday evening in a small office. Eventually, as I went around visiting churches and sharing my story, the group grew to six couples, and Freddie and me.

We watched as the husband of our first couple, changed the direction of his life; attending church regularly, and even becoming a deacon. His countenance changed as joy replaced the despair he experienced at the hands of his drug demons.

He faced the consequences of his past life, with Jesus by his side, beholding the miracle of the court dropping his drug charges and setting him free.

I wish the story could end there, but it doesn't. As time passed, we didn't see the couple very much. They stopped coming to DAP. But I thought about them—particularly the husband—often, promising myself to stop by their house and see them when I got the chance.

I was devastated when I got the news that the husband was dead. OD'd on the bathroom floor of his mother's house, where he and his wife had had to move. He succumbed to his past, using drugs to escape the despair of unemployment and physical pain from a back injury.

His death really shook me up. *I will never again put off opportunities to visit people I know are in need,* I thought to myself. Maybe if I had given him a little time, the husband would still be alive today.

As I shared my story with more and more people, our support group began filling up. Freddie and I eventually opened our own home to have support meetings in, and sometimes there were 30 or 40 people in attendance. The lack of room was acute, and we finally got relief with help from Azure Hills Seventh-day Adventist church, in Grand Terrace, that allowed us to use its fellowship hall. We moved our meetings there, and changed from Saturday night to Tuesday night.

Most of those who attended DAP meetings were drug addicts who were not in recovery, but who wanted help beating their dependencies. Usually, they attended meetings with other family members in tow, most times a wife. Eager to give them something to hold on to, I didn't care if they were high or still using. I just wanted to reach out and help.

Soon, it was apparent that my talking, sharing, praying

approach was not aiding anybody. Even though I was a former drug addict, helping other addicts was a new ball game I knew nothing about. The drug dependents attending our support group loved coming to the meetings. They knew it was okay to get a buzz on, and we'd still take them. The support group evolved into a social gathering, with a couple of guys also coming to deal drugs at one time.

"This isn't right," I told Freddie in discouragement. "We can't do it this way. We're not helping these guys when we allow them to come to the meetings while they're actively using."

"But what can we do?" Freddie had no answers either. We were both lost as to the right direction to follow. As we pondered and discussed our plight, Freddie came up with an idea.

"Maybe we need a therapist."

"I don't know about that, baby," I said a little skeptically. I had never had any good experiences with therapists, and I couldn't get past my initial bias. "Maybe we can start by laying some ground rules."

Freddie agreed with me and we prayed about it. At the next support meeting, I laid down the law.

"If you're on drugs, I don't want you coming here anymore." Some looks of surprise flickered across the faces staring at me.

A little nervous, I continued. "I don't care if we get down to just two of you coming, if you're not sincere, then this isn't the place for you. We want to help you get off drugs, but if that's not what you want to do, then don't come back."

Of course, my ultimatum had the effect we assumed it would. Many people did not come back and the group dwindled to between five and twenty regular attendees. Pretty soon, it leveled off to about a dozen regulars, with new people floating in and out. But those twelve who stayed meant business.

Using a twelve-step program patterned after Alcoholics Anonymous, we began to notice life changes in our members.

Eventually, we did add the services of a therapist who really had a valuable impact on our support group members. But even as we got control of the support group, Freddie and I wanted to offer something more. In the back of our minds, we kept a desire to open a live-in recovery home for drug addicts. Again, not knowing how to go about opening such a place, we put it on the back burner and maintained focus on the support group.

The time came when DAP needed to become a formal non-profit organization. Freddie and I had gotten information previously on becoming a nonprofit, but we'd never followed through. The whole process landed us into unfamiliar territory—creating a board of trustees, a formal budget, and lots of forms to fill out. When we completed the task and turned in the application, we were told it would take at least a year to get approval."

At home, Freddie put the Lord on the situation. "Lord, " she would pray everyday, "we'd like to have our nonprofit status by December. You know what we're trying to accomplish and we know You have the power to speed the process along." On December 29, 1989, DAP became an official nonprofit organization.

— — — — •— — — —

Freddie and I joined a Seventh-day Adventist evangelistic team called "Breath of Life," to minister to drug users attending the religious meetings sponsored by the team. This required us to go out of town for weeks at a time, at least once a year. We loved doing the work, because it allowed our drug ministry to spread all across the nation.

Meanwhile, the support group was not being as effective as

we'd hoped. Seeing the clients, as we started calling them, once a week wasn't enough to make a real difference. It was akin to sending children to school once a week and expecting them to learn at the same pace as those who go daily.

"These guys need around the clock supervision," I told Freddie. I knew from experience, learning how to cope without drugs took constant encouragement and diversion.

"Well," responded Freddie, "we need to open our recovery home."

"But we ain't got nothing," I exclaimed. "No house, no furniture, no beds, nothing."

"Since when is that a problem?" Freddie's faith was taking over, and she was right. We'd seen God work numerous miracles for us already. Why would He stop now? So we started making plans for our live-in recovery home.

By law, we could only have six occupants, so we needed six beds. We wanted a therapist who could work with the clients on a daily basis, one-to-one as well as group counseling. We also thought a work program would keep our clients busy through the day, helping them be productive and fueling their self-esteem.

Once our plans were laid, we presented it to the board of trustees. They would approve opening the recovery home only after we had $14,000 to meet our proposed budget. Now we had our plan, and the board's tentative approval. It was time to watch the Lord go to work.

One evening Freddie was driving one of DAP's board members, Ann, home after a meeting. About seven houses from where we lived, Ann noticed a house for rent. "Freddie, that would make a nice recovery home," she said pointing to the house.

"In this neighborhood?" Shaking her head, Freddie said

"there's no way we could have a recovery home for drug addicts here. They wouldn't allow it." It was difficult to picture our neighbors—professionals living in a middle-class residential area—allowing us to run a recovery home in their midst.

"You might be right, but I feel impressed to tell you to ask about that house," Ann insisted.

"Okay."

When Freddie restated her and Ann's conversation to me, I agreed to go with her to look at the house. It was very nice and appeared to be just what we needed. "I'll give the real estate agent a call," I promised. When I called him, I told him right up front what I wanted.

"My wife and I have looked at a house you have for rent in our neighborhood, and we're interested in renting it to use for a drug recovery program."

He laughed. "No way, sir. We can not have a drug recovery program in your neighborhood."

"We'd still like to fill out an application."

"Sure, if you want to. But I can tell you right now, you won't get it for a recovery home."

We filled out the application and before we turned it in to the real estate agent, we prayed over it. We were heading out of town with Breath of Life for a month, and wouldn't be able to stay on top of it.

"Lord," we asked earnestly, "if this is the house You want us to have for DAP, then you keep it empty for us until we get back in town. If it's not for us, then let it be rented when we return." With that, we gave the real estate agent the application and headed for Detroit.

While we were away, Freddie called the agent, once, to find out the status of the house.

"It's still available," she was informed, "but that's because I haven't been able to reach the owners yet. They live in Germany."

"Well, while you're doing that, would you be interested in having some materials on DAP? At least it will explain our program to you. If you check us out with the neighbors, I'm sure you'll find we have a good reputation. Or, I could send the material to the owners."

"No, you can send them to me and I'll mail it to the owner. But again, I'm sure he won't agree to have his n we returned home. We called our agent, who shared that the house had experienced plumbing problems and all the carpet had to be replaced

"Can we see the new carpet?" Freddie asked.

"Sure. Go on over and I'll meet you there."

We walked through the house, with the agent, admiring the carpet. "It looks really nice," Freddie commented. Then looking straight at the real estate agent, she added "I believe this is the house the Lord is going to give us." The agent didn't laugh this time. "Do you REALLY want the house, I hesitated signing the lease. We still hadn't raised the entire $14,000 needed to cover our proposed budget, the stipulation DAP's board made regarding opening a recovery home. As I paused for about thirty seconds, trying to make a decision, in my head I was saying "Lord, maybe I ought to ask You to hold this house for one more month, and then sign."

"Take it now, or forget it." The agent's voice invaded my inner struggle. The decision was made. We signed. DAP had a house. An empty house, but the first step was complete.

Within a week, we watched the Lord furnish the house. First, a woman who heard my story at Azure Hills Church approached me afterwards and offered to donate to DAP anything left over from her sister-in-law's estate sale. Of course, hardly any furniture sold. As a result we received living room furniture, lamps, and fixtures.

Secondly, Freddie's sister, who'd recently relocated to Florida, couldn't afford to get her furniture out of storage and shipped to her. She offered it to DAP for $800; a set worth at least $3,000.

In the end, we only had to buy six twin beds for the house, which we bought cheap from a Goodwill store.

In 1990, DAP opened its very own live-in recovery home. My life had come full circle. From life, to death, to life again.

Praise the Lord!

Have mercy on me, O God,
according to Your unfailing love; according
to Your great compassion blot out my
transgressions. Wash away all my iniquity
and cleanse me from my sin.
For I know my transgressions, and my sin is
always before me. Against You, You only,
have I sinned and done what is evil
in Your sight,
so that You are proved right when You
speak and justified when You judge me.
Surely I was sinful at birth, sinful from the
time my mother conceived me.
Surely You desire truth in the inner parts;
You teach me wisdom in the inmost place.
Cleanse me with hyssop, and I will be clean;
wash me, and I will be whiter than snow.
Let me hear joy and gladness;
let the bones You have crushed rejoice.
Hide Your face from my sins
and blot out all my iniquity.
Create in me a pure heart, O God,
and renew a steadfast spirit within me.
Do not cast me from Your presence
or take Your Holy Spirit from me. Restore to
me the joy of Your salvation and grant me
a willing spirit, to sustain me.
Then I will teach transgressors Your ways,
and sinners will turn back to You.
Psalms 51:1-13

THANK YOU, JESUS!

DAP

When DAP first opened, the program was three months long. Realizing a need for more time to work with clients, DAP extended the program to one year as of October, 1993.

Although the Drug Alternative Program has seen many clients walk through its doors, only 24 have completed the program—a testament to the severe struggle drug dependents have committing to a life change. Regardless, 50% of DAP's graduates have remained drug free.

As substance abuse refuses to relinquish its hold on America, the need for help has not diminished. It remains so great, the Lord has blessed Clifford and Freddie's ministry by allowing DAP to purchase a second recovery home. This increases DAP's capacity to house and aide 12 clients in their efforts to break their drug cycle.

Cliff and Freddie are available for speaking engagements. For appointment scheduling or for more information on DAP, please write or call:

Drug Alternative Program
11868 Arliss Drive
Grand Terrace, CA 92313

1-800-784-1094 or (909) 783-1094
fax: (909) 783-1098
email: dapcalif@aol.com